THIS STRANGE WILDERNESS

This Strange Wilderness

THE LIFE AND ART OF
JOHN JAMES AUDUBON

Nancy Plain

University of Nebraska Press · Lincoln & London

Publication of this volume was
assisted by a grant from the Friends
of the University of Nebraska Press.

Library of Congress
Cataloging-in-Publication Data
Plain, Nancy.
This strange wilderness:
the life and art of John James
Audubon / Nancy Plain.
pages   cm
Includes bibliographical
references and index.
ISBN 978-0-8032-4884-7 (pbk.: alk. paper)
ISBN 978-0-8032-8401-2 (epub)
ISBN 978-0-8032-8402-9 (mobi)
ISBN 978-0-8032-8403-6 (pdf)
1. Audubon, John James, 1785–1851.
2. Ornithologists—United States—
Biography. 3. Naturalists—United
States—Biography. I. Title. II. Title:
Life and art of John James Audubon.
QL31.A9P65 2015   508.092—dc23
[B]   2014020552

Set in Tribute by Renni Johnson.
Designed by N. Putens.

For my grandchildren

June Rose Evans, Jack Alan Dodge,

and those yet to come,

"with a heart as light as a bird on the wing"

I often think the woods the

only place in which I truly *live*.

JOHN JAMES AUDUBON

Contents

Illustrations

Acknowledgments

Special thanks go to Noah Burg for his generous help with my questions on ornithology and to Bill Markley for sending me valuable information on the western forts. I would also like to thank the New-York Historical Society for its magnificent and inspiring exhibition of Audubon's watercolors. And many thanks go to the following museums and galleries that made this book possible by kindly granting me permission to use images from their collections: the New-York Historical Society; the American Museum of Natural History; the John James Audubon Museum in Henderson, Kentucky; the Museum of Comparative Zoology at Harvard University; the Montana Historical Society; Godel and Company Fine Art in New York, New York; and the Joel Oppenheimer Gallery in Chicago, Illinois.

I have long wanted to write a book about the roving bird artist, so I am grateful beyond words to everyone at the University of Nebraska Press. Alicia Christensen, Tom Swanson, Sabrina Ehmke Sergeant, Rosemary Vestal, Kathryn Owens, Vicki Chamlee, Nathan Putens, and many others at the press have been with me every step of the way.

Introduction

In the heat of the afternoon, the swamp was drowsy and still. Turtles rested on a fallen log. An alligator lazed by the water. High up in a cypress tree, there was a flash of color as a great blue heron smoothed her feathers and settled back on a mossy branch. Only the mosquitoes were busy, swarming and humming in the heavy air.

A gunshot blasted the stillness. Hundreds of birds burst shrieking from the treetops, flying in every direction. All except the great blue heron. She clung to her branch for a second, then tumbled down dead to the water below. The hunter, John James Audubon, shouldered his gun and waded through the swamp to pick up his prey.

That same afternoon he made a painting of the beautiful bird, capturing her jewel-like colors—blue, black, white, a splash of red. He preferred using live birds as models but almost always drew from freshly killed ones instead. These were the days before photography, and he wanted to get every detail right, down to the smallest feather. "My wish to impart truths has been my guide," he wrote, and he signed his pictures "Drawn from Nature, by J. J. Audubon."[1]

Ever since he was a boy, he had been curious about birds and often skipped school to sketch them in the countryside near his home. Now he had set out to do what no one had done before—to paint all the bird species in North America. Many others over the centuries had painted birds. But most of their work seemed stiff and unnatural to Audubon, as if the birds were sitting for their portraits. He thought—no, he knew—that he could do better.

"My Work will be *the* Work indeed!" he declared.[2] And it was. His masterpiece, *The Birds of America*, was a lifetime in the making. It is a magnificent collection of pictures of almost five hundred species—some of them discovered by Audubon himself—and when it was published, the world knew him as one of the greatest bird artists who had ever lived.

Audubon's birds glow with life. They look real enough to hop off the page and fly away. His paintings not only show how the birds look but also tell a story about how they live. A mockingbird defends its eggs from a rattlesnake, a bald eagle clutches a catfish in its claw, a fat little puffin goes for a swim. *The Birds of America* is like a magical visit with all the winged creatures in a vast secret garden.

Born in Haiti and raised in France, Audubon had come to America in 1803, when Thomas Jefferson was president. There were only seventeen states in the Union then, so most of the country was to Americans a mysterious wilderness. Every year explorers set out to chart distant rivers and mountains. Audubon became an explorer, too, looking for birds in their natural habitats. "My whole mind was ever filled with my passion for rambling," he wrote.[3] He loved to wake up before the sun, gather his dog and his gun, and head out into the singing forest. His quest took him all over the North American continent from the Florida Keys to the stormy coast of Labrador and from the New Jersey shore to Indian Country in the Dakotas. He hiked hundreds of miles,

1. *Great Blue Heron* by John James Audubon.

floated down rivers, climbed rocks, and crawled into caves. Once while chasing an owl, he nearly drowned in quicksand. Audubon was a naturalist as well as an artist because he studied everything he could about the birds, from the size of their eggs to the speed of their flight. He even tried to understand their emotional lives. Almost every day he wrote letters and detailed field notes, which he later turned into bird "biographies" and lively tales of the frontier.

Artist. Naturalist. Writer. Hunter and explorer. The far places and the birds called to him. To the end of his life he stayed true to his plan "to search out the things which have been hidden since the creation of this wondrous world."[4]

THIS STRANGE WILDERNESS

No 10. Plate 47. —

Ruby throated Humming-bird. _ Males 1.2.3.4. F. 2 5. 6 . Young

Trochilus Colubris

Plant Bignonia radicans

1 *Beloved Boy*

Hot sun and hummingbirds. Orange trees with dark green leaves. These were some of John James Audubon's earliest memories. He was born a little French boy named Jean Rabin on April 26, 1785, in Haiti. Haiti, then a French colony called Saint-Domingue, forms a part of the island of Hispaniola, set in the warm Caribbean Sea. Jean never knew his mother, Jeanne Rabin. She had come from France to Saint-Domingue to work as a maid and died a few months after Jean was born. His parents had not been married to each other—a fact that he would try to hide all his life—so he was given his mother's last name.

The boy's father, Jean Audubon, was a French sea captain who owned a large sugar plantation on the island. He also bought and sold African slaves. But enslaved Africans far outnumbered white landowners, and during the 1780s, rumblings of an uprising against the brutal system were growing louder every day. So Jean Audubon brought his son and a daughter, Rose, back to his home base in France. There they would be raised by his wife, Anne, who had no children of her own.

2. *Ruby-throated Hummingbird*. Audubon described this bird as a "glittering fragment of the rainbow."

Anne loved them as if they had been hers from the start, and she especially doted on Jean. "She therefore completely spoiled me," he later recalled, "hid my faults, boasted to every one of my youthful merits, and, worse than all, said frequently in my presence that I was the handsomest boy in France."[1] She gave him plenty of pocket money, too, and allowed him to buy whatever he wanted at the candy stores in town. After a few years, the Audubons formally adopted the children. Now Jean had not only a new mother but a new name—Jean-Jacques Audubon.

The family had a home in the city of Nantes in western France and a country house called La Gerbetière in the village of Couëron. Both places were on the banks of the Loire River. In the countryside, young Audubon first learned the joys of rambling. Every morning, his mother packed his lunch basket for school, but he often played hooky instead, running off with his friends to explore meadows and marshes and the banks of the river. After he had eaten his lunch, he would load his basket with "curiosities"—birds' eggs, flowers and mosses, interesting stones.[2] His bedroom began to look like a miniature natural history museum, crammed with small treasures. He felt a bond with nature that grew stronger every year until, as he put it, it bordered on a "frenzy."[3]

Most of all he loved birds. The "feathered tribes," he called them.[4] His father shared this love, and together the two went bird watching, studying the creatures' habits, admiring their graceful flight. When Captain Audubon showed his son a book of bird illustrations, the boy was inspired to draw.

He made pencil outlines and filled in the colors with pastels. At first his birds were just stick figures with heads and tails, and he became frustrated with his "miserable attempts."[5] Even as his work improved,

3. *La Gerbetière*, photograph of Audubon's country house in France.

he thought it was never good enough. "How sorely disappointed did I feel. . . . My pencil gave birth to a family of cripples."[6] Every year on his birthday, he threw hundreds of pictures into a bonfire and vowed to do better.

"A vivid pleasure shone upon those days of my early youth," Audubon would one day remember.[7] Yet there was another side to French life during his childhood. The French Revolution, which had begun in 1789, turned into a nightmare known as the Reign of Terror. In 1793, King Louis XVI and Queen Marie Antoinette were beheaded on the guillotine. One year later, the Terror came to the Audubons' own city, Nantes, and it was worse there than almost anywhere else. The revolutionaries set out to exterminate their enemies, the royalists.

4. *Marsh Wren* by John James Audubon.

Mass shootings and beheadings were common, and the streets came to smell like death. Hundreds of people, many of them priests, were tied up, thrown onto barges, and drowned in the river. In later life, Audubon would write little about these dark days except to say, "The Revolutionists covered the earth with the blood of man, woman, and child."[8]

One day in 1796, Captain Audubon, who was now in the French navy, came back from a long sea voyage. What had his children learned while he was away? he asked. Rose showed how well she could play the piano. Jean-Jacques, who in addition to his school classes was taking private lessons in drawing, fencing, dancing, and music, had almost nothing to show. He hadn't even bothered to put strings on his violin. "I, like a culprit, hung my head," he wrote.[9] His father usually had a temper "like the blast of a hurricane."[10] But this time, he just kissed Rose, hummed a little tune, and left the room.

Early the next morning, Jean-Jacques found himself in a horse-drawn carriage with his suitcase and violin. His father sat silently beside him. As the horses trotted farther and farther from home, Captain Audubon still said nothing, and Jean-Jacques did not know where they were going. After several days they reached the surprise destination— the naval academy in the town of Rochefort. The captain had decided that Jean-Jacques should follow in his father's footsteps and train for a career in the navy. The boy was only eleven years old, but Captain Audubon himself had first gone to sea at age twelve. "My beloved boy, thou art now safe," he said. "I have brought thee here that I may be able to pay constant attention to thy studies."[11] Unlike his wife, he was a practical person and wanted his son to get an education and prepare himself for the future.

5. *Off the Maine Coast* by Thomas Birch, 1835. In Audubon's time, ships like these crossed the ocean.

Jean-Jacques, expert hooky player and adventurer, quickly learned how to shoot, sail, and climb the masts of ships. But he rebelled against the military discipline at Rochefort and the long hours of study. Mathematics, especially, was "hard, dull work."[12] One morning, he decided to escape from his strict math teacher. "I gave him the slip, jumped from the window, and ran off through the gardens."[13] He felt like a young bird fleeing the nest. But in no time he was caught and punished. Later, when he flunked the qualifying test for officer training, his father gave up. The elder Audubon retired from the navy, and father and son returned home.

The Audubons now spent all their time at their country house. Jean-Jacques was a teenager, but he had not forgotten his boyhood passions. "Perhaps not an hour of leisure was spent elsewhere than in woods and fields, and to examine either the eggs, nest, young, or parents of any species of birds constituted my delight."[14]

In 1799, the French Revolution ended, but this did not bring peace to France. A general named Napoleon Bonaparte rose to power, and, mad with dreams of empire, he plunged the weary country into war with the rest of Europe. In the spring of 1803, Napoleon was preparing to invade England, and his already enormous army would need a fresh supply of young men. Audubon was now eighteen. He had survived the revolution, and his father was determined that he should survive Napoleon's wars, too. In his travels, Captain Audubon had stopped in America and bought an estate called Mill Grove in the state of Pennsylvania. He decided to send his son there to escape Napoleon's draft and to start a new life.

That summer Audubon boarded a ship bound for America. "I received light and life in the New World," he wrote, and now he was heading back.[15] His mother cried when the ship sailed away, and the young man watched as the coastline of France faded into the distance. "My heart sunk within me. . . . My affections were with those I had left behind, and the world seemed to me a great wilderness."[16]

2 *America, My Country*

Audubon sat in a small cave, watching a grayish brown bird, an eastern phoebe, as she sat on her nest. At first her mate had tried to chase him away, darting and scolding. But he had returned every morning until both birds had grown used to him. Now he was able to peek at the first newly laid egg. "So white and so transparent," he wrote, "that to me the sight was more pleasant than if I had met with a diamond of the same size."[1] Soon five eggs hatched, and five baby birds jostled each other in the nest. They allowed Audubon to touch them. When they were old enough, he picked up each one and gently tied a silver thread around a tiny leg. The phoebes would fly south for the winter, but the threads would show him if any came back to the same spot in the spring.

The next April he heard cries of "fee-bee, fee-bee!" Were these the same "little pilgrims" that he knew?[2] He searched for silver-threaded birds and found two nesting nearby. The experiment had worked. This was the first time that birds were banded in America. No older than twenty, Audubon had just made a major contribution to the study of bird migration and to *ornithology*, or the study of birds, in general.

6. *Eastern Phoebe*. Audubon called phoebes Pewee Flycatchers.

The phoebes' cave was on the banks of the Perkiomen Creek, a stream that flowed through the estate of Mill Grove, Audubon's new American home. His father had chosen the property well. Not far from Philadelphia, Mill Grove was a lovely place—a big stone house on two hundred acres of lawn and orchard, forest and field. An underground vein of lead had been discovered on the land, too, and Captain Audubon hoped to develop it into a mine. Not so his son. Young Audubon was happy just to wander the countryside "with as little concern for the future as if the world had been made for me."[3] Along the creek and on old Indian trails, he hunted for all kinds of woodland animals to draw, but as always, he looked mostly for birds—wild turkeys, ducks, geese, eagles, and more.

It did not take long for Audubon to think of Mill Grove as a "blessed spot" or to adopt the motto "America, My Country."[4] He worked hard at learning English, although he would always speak with a French accent. And he changed his name from the French Jean-Jacques Audubon to the American version—John James Audubon.

He set up a drawing studio at Mill Grove but was as disgusted as ever with his bird pictures. Many of them were flat profiles, done in the tradition of the ornithologists of his day. Others were sketches of birds that he had shot and hung upside down on a string—more like signs for a poultry shop than art, he thought. How could he pose his birds to look alive? The solution came to him in a dream one night, and he jumped out of bed before dawn to try it out.

First he made a "position board" out of a piece of wood, then drove into it sharp wires that could pierce a bird's body and hold it in any position. He tested the device with a newly killed bird called a king-fisher, arranging and rearranging its head, tail, and feet until his fingers

7. *Mill Grove Farm, Perkiomen Creek, Pennsylvania* by Thomas Birch, c. 1820.

bled. "At last—there stood before me the *real* Kingfisher."[5] Now it was time to draw. In order to get the proportions right, he had drawn a network of lines on the position board and a matching grid on his paper. "I outlined the bird, aided by compasses and my eyes, colored it, finished it, without a thought of hunger. . . . This was what I shall call my first drawing actually from nature."[6] The new method was a turning point for Audubon and his art, and he would use it for the rest of his life.

Soon after he fell in love with America, he fell in love with a girl named Lucy Bakewell. The eldest of six children, she was seventeen years old to his nineteen, and she lived across the road from him in a white-columned mansion called Fatland Ford. Her family, the Bakewells, had just emigrated from England. When Audubon first met Lucy, she was sewing by her parlor fire. He was struck by her friendly ways and the "grace and beauty" of her figure, and he believed—rightly—that she admired him as well.[7] "I measured five feet ten and a half inches, was of a fair mien, and [had] quite a handsome figure."[8] He was especially proud of his strength—his "muscles of steel"—and his wavy brown hair, which hung down to his shoulders.[9] John became a frequent visitor to Fatland Ford. The two young people played music together, with Lucy on piano and John on violin or flute. They rode horseback, walked in the woods, and visited John's hideaway, the phoebes' cave. In the cave, they first talked about marriage.

While Lucy was modest and sensible, John was anything but. "I was what in plain terms may be called extremely extravagant," he wrote.[10] On an allowance from his father, he bought the best horses and dogs and fancy guns decorated with silver. "I was ridiculously fond of dress," he added.[11] Even to go hunting—often with Lucy's youngest brother, Billy, tagging along—John wore black satin breeches, silk stockings, and a ruffled shirt. He was also a fearless natural athlete who never missed a chance to show off: "Not a ball, a skating-match, a house or riding party took place without me."[12] One day another Bakewell brother, Tom, dared Audubon to shoot a hole in his hat while skating by at top speed. "Off I went like lightning," Audubon recalled, and when the hat was thrown into the air, he shot it so full of holes it looked like a sieve.[13] A neighbor observed that Audubon was not only the fastest skater he had ever seen, able to leap over gaping holes in the ice, but also the best dancer: "All the ladies wished him as a partner."[14] No wonder Lucy's father, William Bakewell, thought that John was "too young and too useless to be married."[15]

Audubon's own father agreed. So in 1805 John sailed back to France to convince him to change his mind. He stayed for one year. Much of that time he spent hunting for birds in his old childhood haunts with a neighbor, Dr. Charles d'Orbigny. A naturalist and bird expert, d'Orbigny taught John how to conduct his bird studies in a scientific way—how to weigh and measure, how to dissect, and how to classify the different species. This type of classification, called *taxonomy*, was new to ornithology, and ideas about it were constantly changing.

Audubon would return to America with a deeper understanding of the feathered tribes. He would also return with a business partner, a Frenchman named Ferdinand Rozier. Both Mr. Bakewell and Captain Audubon had advised John to become a businessman, serious and responsible at last. Only then would he win their permission to marry. This time when Audubon left France, he wasn't sad. He couldn't wait to see Lucy again.

In 1807 he sold his share of Mill Grove to fund a general store, which he and Rozier planned to locate somewhere in Kentucky. Kentucky was then a frontier state in the "Western country," on the very edge of the unknown. Only twenty-four years had passed since the end of the American Revolution. And only four years since Thomas Jefferson had made the Louisiana Purchase, doubling the size of the country. There were no states at all west of the Kentucky border, yet Americans were moving to Kentucky to build towns and farm its fertile land.

The future storekeepers set out from Pennsylvania in late August on what would be a rough trip. They trudged through the rain on horseback and endured long days in stagecoaches that bogged down in

8. *Wild Turkey*. Like Benjamin Franklin, Audubon wanted the turkey to be named the national bird.

9. (*left*) *John James Audubon* by Frederick Cruikshank, 1831. The artist as he looked in middle age.

10. (*right*) *Lucy Bakewell Audubon* by Frederick Cruikshank, 1835.

the mud. But Audubon loved it all. Moving through ancient, towering forests, surrounded by an orchestra of birdsong, he fell under a kind of spell. "Who is the stranger to my own dear country that can form an adequate conception of the extent of its primeval woods[?]"[16]

They reached the Ohio River at Pittsburgh, loaded their supplies onto a flatboat, and started downriver. In those days before the steamboat, flatboats—raftlike crafts with squared ends—were the best way to move cargo and people on the nation's waterways. The boats had no sails but floated with the current or were pushed along by means of long poles thrust into the riverbed. Audubon's flatboat was carrying everything from hogs to horses, plows to spinning wheels—and whole families of pioneers. Gliding downstream, Audubon was enchanted by the clear, calm river, the untouched forests on shore. At night he saw the moon reflected in black water and heard owls sweep by on quiet wings.

When Audubon and Rozier reached Louisville, Kentucky, they decided to stay. High on a bluff overlooking the river, the town was already a busy port—the right place to open a general store. The partners rented space and set out their goods, everything from bacon to gunpowder.

John had finally won approval from both fathers to marry Lucy. So he made the long trip back to Pennsylvania for his wedding, which was held on April 5, 1808. The day after the ceremony, he and Lucy started back to Louisville. Along the way, their stagecoach overturned. Lucy was thrown from it and badly bruised, but she had no thought of turning back. Although wealthy and well educated, she was not afraid to try the pioneers' life. She and John were travelers in the new nation, and they saw their future on the frontier.

3 *The American Woodsman*

Owning a store did not keep Audubon from his wandering ways. While Ferdinand Rozier stood behind the counter all day, Audubon took to the woods. "Birds were birds then as now," he later wrote, "and my thoughts were ever and anon turning toward them as the objects of my greatest delight. I shot, I drew, I looked on nature only; my days were happy beyond human conception, and beyond this I really cared not."[1] The only parts of the business that he enjoyed were the buying trips that took him back through the "darling forests," back to the big cities of Philadelphia and New York.[2] These trips provided the perfect excuse for bird watching; once he lost sight of his packhorses because he was tracking the flight of a certain warbler. As her husband's collection of drawings grew, Lucy confided in one of her sisters, "If I were jealous, I would have a bitter time of it, for every bird is my rival."[3]

Lucy and John lived in a Louisville boardinghouse called the Indian Queen. There in 1809 their son Victor Gifford was born. The Audubons were popular in the frontier town—Lucy for her gentleness and learning, John for his hunting skills and general love of a good time. On coming to Kentucky, he had put away his black satin clothes and put on buckskin and moccasins instead. He carried his gunpowder in a buffalo horn and stuck a tomahawk in his belt. Gone was the country gentleman of Mill Grove. He thought of himself now as the "American Woodsman."

One day in 1810 an unexpected visitor came to the store. He was Alexander Wilson, a Scotsman and the most famous ornithologist in America at the time. "How well do I remember him, as he then walked up to me!" Audubon wrote.[4] Wilson had a "peculiar look," with his long nose and piercing eyes.[5] Tucked under his arm was part of his life's work, a collection of bird drawings and descriptions titled *American Ornithology*. He asked Audubon to subscribe to it, to make payments as new volumes were completed. Audubon was about to sign up when Rozier stopped him. "Your drawings are certainly far better," he said in French, "and again you must know as much of the habits of American birds as this gentleman."[6] Audubon had to agree.

By this time he had completed about two hundred drawings of birds, all of them life-size. The woods were Audubon's art school. Everything he drew, he had seen himself—unlike many other ornithologists, who worked from stuffed specimens. And almost everything he knew, he had taught himself. His only scientific book was one by Carl Linnaeus, the founder of modern taxonomy.

11. *John James Audubon* by John James Audubon, 1826. Pencil on paper. He sketched himself as the American Woodsman.

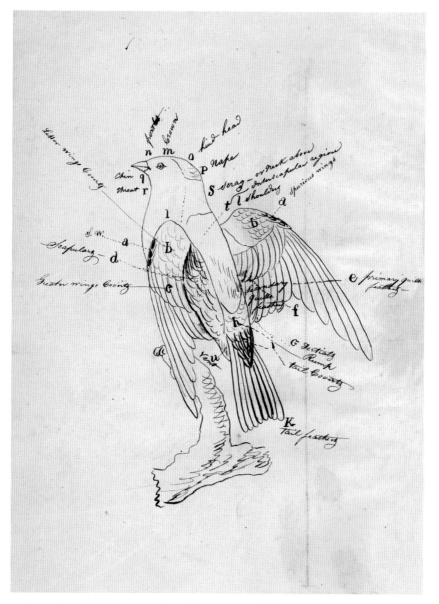

12. *Drawing of Bird Anatomy* by John James Audubon.

When Wilson saw Audubon's pictures, he was astonished. How had this backwoods shopkeeper taught himself to draw so well? And how had he managed to find species that Wilson himself had never seen? He asked Audubon if he planned to publish his work. Audubon said no because he was still intent on running the store. But the idea of publishing took hold in his mind and never let go. From that day on, Audubon knew that Wilson was the ornithologist to beat. In the years to come, he would compare his birds with the Scotsman's, checking for similarities, checking for—and sometimes finding—Wilson's mistakes.

Louisville was settling up fast. As more merchants came to town, Audubon and Rozier faced competition. So they moved a hundred miles down the Ohio to set up a new shop in Henderson, Kentucky. Henderson was just a huddle of log cabins then, with few customers for any store. But Audubon was happy. He always longed for a "wilder range."[7]

In the winter of 1810, he and Rozier started on an expedition to Ste. Genevieve, a village near St. Louis, Missouri. This time they traveled by keelboat—a cargo boat with a keel and pointed ends—first down the Ohio, then up the Mississippi River. All the way, the passengers battled snowstorms, ferocious cold, and solid masses of ice. Audubon smiled to see how Rozier endured the trip, "wrapped in a blanket, like a squirrel in winter quarters with his tail about his nose."[8] He himself was having the time of his life.

Wherever the keelboat tied up to shore, Audubon went exploring. Once he spied a brownish-black eagle, which he called the Bird of Washington in honor of the first president. He was sure he had discovered a new species, but the bird was actually a young bald eagle that had not yet grown its distinctive white head feathers. On another

13. *Trumpeter Swan*. Audubon watched swans toss water over their backs "in sparkling globules, like so many large pearls."

side trip, a party of Shawnee Indians took Audubon to a lake where there were "swans by the hundreds, and as white as rich cream, either dipping their black bills in the water, or stretching out one leg on the surface, or gently floating along."[9]

The expedition proved to be the last straw for Rozier. When the keelboat reached Ste. Genevieve, he decided to stay, and the partnership of Audubon and Rozier broke up. Rozier complained that "Audubon had no taste for commerce, and was continually in the forest."[10] Audubon would never deny it: "I seldom passed a day without drawing a bird, or noting something respecting its habits."[11] But he summed up his opinion of his ex-partner this way: "Rozier cared only for money."[12]

Audubon traveled overland back to his family in Henderson, a distance of 165 miles. "Winter was just bursting into spring. . . . The prairies began to be dotted with beauteous flowers, abounded with deer, and my own heart was filled with happiness at the sights before me."[13]

He claimed that he was almost murdered along the way. His story about the strange incident is called "The Prairie." It is one of the many "episodes"—some true, some tall tales—that he would write.

Following an Indian trail, Audubon came to a cabin where he hoped to spend the night. The owner, a gruff pioneer woman, invited him in. By the fire sat a young Indian, whose face was bloody from a wound he had gotten when his arrow backfired into his eye. The wounded man did not speak to Audubon but kept glancing with his good eye at the woman, as if to warn Audubon that she was dangerous. After she admired Audubon's watch, which hung on a gold chain around his neck, the Indian's warnings grew stronger. "He passed and repassed me several times, and once pinched me on the side so violently, that the pain nearly brought forth an exclamation of anger."[14] In the dead of night, the woman's two sons came home. Pretending to be asleep, Audubon heard the three plotting to kill the Indian and himself in order to steal the watch. Then he heard a knife being sharpened, and "cold sweat covered every part of my body."[15] He silently prepared to fire his gun in self-defense. Just then "two stout travelers, each with a long rifle on his shoulder," burst in.[16] When they heard Audubon's story, they helped him tie up the would-be killers. The next morning, the travelers dispensed frontier justice—were the cabin dwellers hanged or shot?—and burned the cabin to the ground. Audubon and the others went their separate ways. During all his wanderings, Audubon writes, "this was the only time at which my life was in danger from my fellow creatures."[17]

14. (*left*) *Victor Gifford Audubon* by John James Audubon, 1823.
15. (*right*) *John Woodhouse Audubon* by John James Audubon, 1823.

Back in Henderson, he formed a new partnership with Lucy's brother Tom. Tom went to New Orleans, where he planned to sell goods imported from England. The venture failed soon after it started, though, because the War of 1812 between America and England put a stop to all trade between the two countries. But the store in Henderson thrived. Lucy and John bought a house with several acres of meadow and a pond for ducks and geese. They even kept a pet turkey, with a red ribbon tied around its neck. "The pleasures which I have felt at Henderson and under the roof of that log cabin, can never be effaced from my heart until after death," wrote Audubon.[18] In 1812 the Audubons' second son, John Woodhouse (Johnny), was born, and now there were two "Kentucky lads" to raise.

Audubon's horse, Barro, was a scruffy little mustang that had once belonged to an Osage Indian. One afternoon, as Audubon trotted Barro through the countryside, the sky darkened, and he heard what sounded like "the distant rumbling of a violent tornado."[19] He tried to kick Barro into a gallop, but the horse "fell a-groaning piteously, hung his head, spread out his four legs, as if to save himself from falling, and stood stock still, continuing to groan."[20] Audubon thought that Barro was dying, when suddenly—earthquake! "The ground rose and fell . . . like the ruffled waters of a lake. . . . I had never witnessed anything of the kind before. . . . Who can tell of the sensations which I experienced when I found myself rocking as it were on my horse, and with him moved to and fro like a child in a cradle . . . ?"[21] When the rocking stopped, horse and rider raced home faster than they had ever run before. They had just survived one of the New Madrid earthquakes, a series of quakes that were the strongest ever recorded in the eastern United States.

Another time the sky grew dark not because of an earthquake but because a flock of passenger pigeons was flying overhead. In Audubon's time, these birds owned the skies. There were billions of them, more than all other American bird species combined, and one flock could take three days to pass by. Audubon describes a scene in which men assembled with poles and guns to kill the birds for food for their hogs:

Suddenly there burst forth a general cry of "Here they come!" The noise which they made, though yet distant, reminded me of a hard gale at sea. . . . As the birds arrived and passed over me, I felt a current of air that surprised me. Thousands were soon knocked down by the pole-men. The birds continued to pour in. The fires were lighted, and a magnificent, as well as wonderful

16. *Passenger Pigeon*. The last known passenger pigeon died in 1914 in a Cincinnati zoo. Her name was Martha.

and almost terrifying, sight presented itself. The Pigeons, arriving by thousands, alighted everywhere, one above another, until solid masses . . . were formed on the branches all round. Here and there the perches gave way under the weight with a crash, and, falling to the ground, destroyed hundreds of the birds beneath. . . . It was a scene of uproar and confusion. I found it quite useless to speak, or even to shout to those persons who were nearest to me. Even the reports of the guns were seldom heard, and I was made aware of the firing only by seeing the shooters reloading.

No one dared venture within the line of devastation.[22]

Few people then thought that these birds could ever become extinct. But Audubon predicted correctly that they would and not from mass slaughter but from loss of habitat. As America's infinite forests fell to the settler's ax, the pigeon population disappeared. "Here, again, the tyrant of the creation, man, interferes," wrote Audubon.[23]

The young Audubon family was growing up with the country, and Kentucky was home. John was free to roam its woods, hunt birds, and practice his art. In 1815 a new baby, Lucy, was born. "This Place saw My best days, My Happiest," he would recall.[24]

But soon his happiness turned to sorrow. Baby Lucy died at age two. And there were more troubles to come. Audubon and Tom Bakewell had built a large steam mill in Henderson, but it "worked worse and worse every day" until it finally failed, sinking Audubon in a swamp of debt.[25] A man who owed him money beat him viciously with a club, and Audubon had to stab his attacker—not fatally—in self-defense. Then in 1819 a nationwide financial panic ended Audubon's chances of recovering his business losses. He and Lucy sold the store and almost everything they owned to pay their bills. Lucy "felt the pangs of our misfortunes perhaps more heavily than I," Audubon wrote, "but never for an hour lost her courage."[26]

Without the store, he had to find a new way to make a living. Taking only the clothes on his back, his drawings, his dog, and his gun, he walked to Louisville in hopes of finding a job. Along the way, he was "Poor & Miserable of thoughts."[27] For the first time in his life, he had no interest in the birds that clucked, sang, strutted, and sailed through the forest around him. They "all looked like enemies, and I turned my eyes from them, as if I could have wished that they had never existed."[28]

4 *Down the Mississippi*

When Audubon reached Louisville, he was arrested and thrown into jail for his debts. He declared bankruptcy and was set free, but he had no place to go. Nicholas Berthoud, the husband of Lucy's sister Eliza, took him in. The Berthouds lived in the nearby village of Shippingport, and Lucy and the boys soon joined Audubon there. In Shippingport, Lucy had another baby girl, whom she named Rose. But Rose, too, died, only months later. The Audubons' lives really had hit bottom, yet John refused to accept defeat. "Was I inclined to cut my throat in foolish despair? No!! I *had* talents, and to them I instantly resorted."[1]

He began drawing portraits in black chalk for five dollars apiece. Louisville citizens liked them, and Audubon was able to raise his prices. Out around town and country he rode, paid even to capture last images of people on their deathbeds. One clergyman disinterred his dead son for a portrait, "which, by the way," the artist noted, "I gave to the parents as if [the boy were] still alive, to their intense satisfaction."[2]

Although he was working to keep his family off the "starving list," he sometimes skipped a portrait job to draw a bird.[3] In troubled times, birds and forest solitude comforted him best, and he often had to force himself to return to the company of people.

17. *Bonaparte's Gull.* Audubon painted each gull separately, then brought them together in a collage.

When the demand for portraits in Louisville dried up, Audubon took a job in Ohio at the new Western Museum at Cincinnati College. It was one of America's first natural history museums. There he worked as a taxidermist, stuffing birds and fish for wildlife displays. He also started a small drawing school. But in his spare time, it was still "I shot, I drew, I looked on nature only."[4] On one outing, he saw a pair of Bonaparte's gulls, "sweeping gracefully over the tranquil waters" of the Ohio River, and he visited a colony of cliff swallows, whose odd nests looked like a cluster of mud pots stuck sideways onto rock.[5]

Dr. Daniel Drake, president of Cincinnati College, gave Audubon space to exhibit his drawings. He recognized that the collection included many species never pictured before. Drake's praise—and the example of Alexander Wilson's bird book—inspired Audubon to come up with his own "Great Idea."[6] He would explore the country to study and paint every bird species in its natural habitat. And he would publish his findings in a major work to be called *The Birds of America*. This would make him what he already knew he could be—the greatest ornithologist in America.

It was a risky plan. It seemed crazy. Audubon was already thirty-six years old, and Lucy's relatives were furious. How could he even *think* of leaving his family to tramp around after birds? And how could he possibly find every species? But Lucy believed that John could succeed. She promised to support herself and the boys by teaching while John was gone. Audubon himself had no money. "My Talents are to be My Support and My enthusiasm My Guide."[7]

On October 12, 1820, he boarded another flatboat and traveled south by way of the Ohio and Mississippi Rivers. He was bound for New Orleans and the waterways of Louisiana, where millions of migrating

18. *Cliff Swallow*. A young bird peeks out of its mud nest.

birds spent the winter. The flatboat crew was a bunch of rowdy young men. Meals were mostly bacon and biscuits, and Audubon's bed was a buffalo robe spread out on deck. In his bags were his book on taxonomy, some volumes by Wilson, rolls of drawing paper, a box of art supplies, his flute, his fiddle, and a journal that he would write in every day. In his wallet were letters of introduction that he and Lucy had collected from their Kentucky congressman, Henry Clay, and from William Henry Harrison, the future president. These letters were the nineteenth century's version of social networking, and Audubon planned to present them to influential people in New Orleans.

He had also brought along his most talented art student, a Cincinnati boy named Joseph Mason. Mason's father had given him permission to go, along with a gift of five dollars. Although the boy was only thirteen, he would be Audubon's assistant and paint backgrounds—flowers and plants—for the bird pictures.

It was Audubon's favorite season on the Ohio. A golden mist hung in the air. The riverbank blazed with fall colors, and "every tree was hung with long and flowing festoons of different species of vines, many loaded with clustered fruits of varied brilliancy."[8] When the boat reached Henderson, Kentucky, Audubon sent other men to pick up his dog, Dash, who had been left behind with neighbors. The thought of returning to the scene of his business failures made Audubon's blood run cold.

Because he couldn't afford to pay for the ride, he had signed on as the boat's hunter. There were no supermarkets in 1820, so most Americans who wanted meat had to find it for themselves. Audubon and Mason often rowed to shore in a small skiff to shoot turkeys or ducks for dinner, as well as deer, squirrels, and opossums. They kept a sharp eye out for any bears that might be lurking in the woods.

At the place where the Ohio joins the big Mississippi, two Indians paddled by in a canoe, and Audubon wrote, "Here the Traveller enters a New World."[9] This was bird country—the great Mississippi River Flyway, one of the busiest migration routes in the world. Long, V-shaped lines of birds streamed by overhead, all going south for the winter. There were Canada geese and trumpeter swans. Sandhill cranes and cormorants. Flocks of gulls gathered on islands in the river. And blackbirds zipped past, "forming a Line Like disbanded Soldiers all anxious to reach the point of destination."[10] In the woods, Audubon spotted red-tailed hawks, ivory-billed woodpeckers, and Carolina parakeets. The colorful little parakeets, a type of parrot, were the only parrots native to North America. But because they liked to feast on crops, farmers were shooting them by the thousands. Audubon worried—and rightly so—that they would soon become extinct.

He shot and drew from first light to candlelight. Neither the rocking of the boat nor the crowded quarters stopped him. He felt like a migrating bird himself, although his mood seesawed between high excitement and the "blue devils" of homesickness and doubt.[11] With every day that passed, he wrote, "the Stronger my Anxiety to see My familly again presses on my mind—and Nothing but the astonishing desire I have of Compleating my work keeps my Spirits at par."[12]

January 7, 1821, and "*New Orleans* at Last."[13] It was a Sunday, and Audubon stepped ashore to the ringing of church bells. The city was the capital of Louisiana, which had become a state only nine years before. At the mouth of the Mississippi River, New Orleans was a booming port town. Its levees and markets were alive with tradesmen, merchants, and planters and with visitors from all over the world—an exotic jumble of languages and faces. Steamboats, the newest mode of

19. *Carolina Parakeet*. This bird has been extinct since the 1920s.

river travel, carried away cotton and sugar from southern plantations and returned with goods from almost everywhere else. New Orleans was also a major center for the slave trade. The rich economy of the American South was built on the backs of the enslaved.

Audubon was ragged and wild looking after his long trip, but he slung his portfolio over his shoulder and took to the streets, looking for work. He bumped into some old acquaintances but was greeted coldly. Then his pocket was picked, and he began to despair. "I rose early tormented by many desagreable thoughts, nearly again without a cent, in a Busling City where no one cares a fig for a Man in my Situation."[14] Yet within a couple of weeks, he had found customers for portraits and some drawing students, too. Sometimes he made enough money to send some home to Lucy. At other times, he couldn't even afford a new journal to write in. One of his drawing pupils was a pretty young woman. Her husband believed that Audubon was flirting with her, so he fired the artist without paying for any past lessons. This was not the only time Audubon had been accused of flirting, although he protested, "Seldom before My coming to New Orleans did *I* think that I was Looked on so favourably by the *fair* sex."[15]

20. *Carolina Parrot* by Alexander Wilson. Wilson's parakeet (*top*) is very different from Audubon's.

Audubon and Joseph Mason lived in dingy, rented rooms. Dinner was often just a hunk of bread and a piece of cheese, one piece so old that maggots popped out of it and made "astounding Leaps" around the table.[16] The two artists were so busy scraping together a living that they had little time to explore the countryside around New Orleans. But birds were sold in the marketplace, and many species lived within the city itself. There were cuckoos, their voices "Loud and Sweet and their Movements elegantly airy."[17] There were yellow-breasted chats, which turned fantastic somersaults in midair during mating season. Warblers sang among the pink magnolias. Often Mason spent whole days drawing flowers, and Audubon noted, "He now *draws Flowers* better than any man probably in America."[18] Audubon himself made wonderful pictures in New Orleans. A great egret, ghostlike against the night sky. A whooping crane, chasing a snack of baby alligator.

Yet Audubon could still write that he was "very much fatigued" of the city.[19] He had not found many new species. And he felt slighted by the city's important men. Once when he asked a well-known painter for a recommendation, he was kept waiting, then told to lay out his drawings on a dirty floor. Most of all, Audubon missed Lucy and wanted her to come to him. But she refused to leave her secure teaching job only to face poverty in New Orleans. Husband and wife exchanged angry letters. "Thou art, not, it seems, as daring as I am about Leaving one place to go to another. . . . I am sorry for that," wrote John.[20] For a moment, he was tempted to abandon *The Birds of America*.

Then he met Mrs. Pirrie.

21. *Great Egret*. The egret was hunted almost to extinction for its feathers. Some of America's earliest bird protection laws were passed to save it.

Yellow-breasted Chat Males 1.2.3.4. F. 5.
Icteria viridis. — Plant Vulgo Sweet Briar.

5 *On the Wing*

Lucretia Pirrie was the wife of James Pirrie, the owner of a cotton plantation called Oakley. The Pirries had a fifteen-year-old daughter, Eliza. Since there were no schools near Oakley, Mrs. Pirrie invited Audubon to work there for a while as Eliza's tutor. He would be paid sixty dollars a month, and his duties would be light. With no better plans before him, he couldn't say no.

Oakley was located north of New Orleans in West Feliciana Parish (a Louisiana *parish* is similar to a county). When Audubon and Mason arrived, they felt as if they had entered another world. The land was hilly, the soil red. Spanish moss hung from oaks and cypress trees, giving the countryside a dark and haunted look. Best of all were the sweet magnolia woods, home to countless birds. It was June, mating time for the winged creatures—what Audubon called the "love season." The air echoed with song.

Oakley plantation house was cool inside, shaded from the heat by trees and shuttered windows. The two wandering artists settled in. For

22. *Yellow-breasted Chat.* During mating season, the chat shows off with aerial acrobatics.

half the day, Audubon instructed "My Lovely Miss Pirrie" in drawing, dancing, music, math, and even the art of making decorative objects out of braided hair.[1] The rest of the day was his. He hiked through woods and fields and slogged through swamps, armed with a stick big enough to fend off alligators. The Feliciana country was also on the Mississippi River Flyway, so there were many thousands of birds—robins and wrens, hawks and herons, woodpeckers and kites. Before Audubon drew a bird, he would spend days observing it and taking notes. "Nature *must* be seen first alive, and well studied, before attempts are made at representing it," he believed.[2] He wanted to know everything—what the birds ate, where they slept, how they found their mates and cared for their young. Because he thought of birds' inner lives in terms of human emotions, he was interested in their personalities, too. Were they meek or fierce, shy or sociable? Blue jays ate other birds' eggs, so according to Audubon, they were thieves and mischief makers—not unlike some people he knew.

He also thought of birdcalls in human terms—the cry of the bald eagle was like the "laugh of a maniac."[3] He could identify every bird by listening, so when he heard an unfamiliar call, he suspected that it came from an unknown species. Most of the new species that he discovered, he

23. *Yellow-breasted Chat* by Mark Catesby. Catesby, an English naturalist, painted American birds in the 1700s.

24. *Blue Jay* by John James Audubon.

would find in Feliciana. This corner of the world became his favorite place, and he called it Happyland.

When he walked into Happyland, he walked in with his gun. "You must be aware," he once wrote, "that I call birds few, when I shoot less than one hundred per day."[4] By obtaining many specimens of a single species, he could better understand the general characteristics of that species. After he drew a bird, his work as a naturalist began. First he measured every part of the bird, even the length of its tongue. Then he dissected it, examining its organs and the contents of its stomach. Male and female of a species, young and old—Audubon the naturalist wanted to know his subjects literally inside and out.

"The naturalist . . . ought to be an artist also."[5] Ever since the trip down the Mississippi, Audubon had been experimenting with color, and in Louisiana, his genius began to shine. He used pastel and watercolor together, layering and blending them, rubbing the colors with his finger or a piece of cork to create effects as rich and soft as feathers. He added other media, too. Pencil or black ink was perfect for delicate things such as spider webs or the legs of a bug. Oil paint formed a tree branch here, a cloud there. Gold metallic paint was just right for the flash of a feather, clear glaze for the gleam of an eye. This mix was something new in painting—a revolution quietly taking shape among the magnolias.

Louisiana was full of snakes, as well as birds. One of Audubon's most startling pictures, done at Oakley, shows a confrontation between four mockingbirds and a rattlesnake. The snake, coiled in a tree, is poised to strike while the birds, which Audubon admired for their "undaunted courage," defend their eggs.[6] The artist used as his model a dead rattler almost six feet long. With Eliza Pirrie sketching next to him, he worked on the drawing for sixteen hours in the summer heat. He always liked

25. *Northern Mockingbird*. This picture caused years of controversy among ornithologists.

to finish a picture at one sitting, but this time he couldn't—the stench became too strong. The finished picture, *Northern Mockingbird*, is only one of many scenes in which Audubon shows the natural world as a place where every living thing must struggle to survive.

Mrs. Pirrie began to think that Eliza was starting to like her tutor a little too much. She told Audubon to leave, allowing him only ten days to organize and pack all his notes and drawings. When he asked to be paid for some classes that his pupil had missed, Mrs. Pirrie flew into a rage. Humiliated, Audubon was not sad to leave "the Ladies of Oakley." But it was "not so with the sweet Woods around us, to leave them was painfull."[7] He and Joseph caught a steamboat back to New Orleans.

In the city once again, Audubon cut his hair—his "horse's mane"— and bought a good suit of clothes.[8] He hoped that his new look would be more pleasing to the respectable folk he met on the street. He listed all he had accomplished since leaving Cincinnati: "62 Drawings of *Birds & Plants*, 3 quadrupeds, 2 Snakes, 50 Portraits of all sorts."[9] But he was lonelier than ever and missed his family so much that he wrote in his journal, "Wished myself off this Miserable Stage."[10] Lucy had finally promised to join him, but she wouldn't say when. Then on December 18, 1821, she did arrive, along with twelve-year-old Victor and Johnny, nine. After a year of separation, the Audubons were together again, living in a tiny house on Dauphine Street.

Lucy still had to support the family. She worked as a governess in New Orleans, then found a teaching job—and a home for her sons—at Beech Woods, another plantation in Feliciana. Jane Percy, an outspoken widow, was its owner. There Lucy set up a little school, which attracted children from the surrounding countryside, and she was soon beloved in the community. Her husband, however, was looked

26. *Black-billed Cuckoo*. The cuckoos are hard to spot among the magnolias.

on by some as an eccentric, even a "madman."[11] "My wife and family alone gave me encouragement," wrote John.[12]

Even after Lucy had come to Louisiana, Audubon and Mason continued as itinerant artists. One of the best pictures from their travels is the *Black-billed Cuckoo*—bird by Audubon, flowers and leaves by Mason. By 1822 Joseph had been traveling with Audubon for two years and had painted about fifty backgrounds for his teacher. His father had died while he was away, and he now decided that it was time to go home. So ended one of America's finest art collaborations, although when Audubon published his work, he would give Mason no credit.

Jane Percy hired Audubon to paint a portrait of her daughters, but it seemed that fighting with his employers was becoming a habit. When Mrs. Percy complained that he had made her daughters' skin look too yellow, it was Audubon's turn to fly into a rage. How dare anyone criticize him, of all people, on *color*! He was immediately kicked off the property.

But he had painted one masterpiece after another in Louisiana, and he believed that it was time to find a publisher. In 1824 he set out to try his luck in Philadelphia, the nation's center of art, science, and learning. Somewhere on the journey north, he wrote to his old business partner: "I am yet, my dear Rozier, on the wing and God only knows how long I may yet remain so."[13]

It was spring when he arrived. He soon found friends and admirers, including the famous portrait painter Thomas Sully and the ornithologist Charles Lucien Bonaparte, nephew of the emperor Napoleon. But Alexander Wilson, who had died in 1813, was still recognized in Philadelphia as the greatest ornithologist, and when Audubon dared to criticize him, he made some powerful enemies. They mocked Audubon as the "trader naturalist," called his work "ill-drawn."[14]

27. *Northern Bobwhite and Red-shouldered Hawk.* Audubon painted many
scenes of birds fighting to survive.

Audubon's bitterest foe was a man named George Ord, Wilson's biographer and editor. Ord prevented the newcomer from joining Philadelphia's prestigious Academy of Natural Sciences. Worse, he made sure that Audubon could find no publisher in the city. Turned away by the men he called the "Philadelphia Sharks," Audubon made a new plan.[15] He would publish his work overseas, in England.

It would take him and Lucy a year to save enough money for this next trip. Mrs. Percy had forgiven him, so he lived at Beech Woods, teaching drawing, French, fencing, and music. And even a dance called the cotillion:

> I placed all the gentlemen in a line reaching across the hall, thinking to give the young ladies time to compose themselves and get ready when called. How I toiled before I could get one graceful step or motion! I broke my bow and nearly my violin in my excitement and impatience! The gentlemen were soon fatigued. The ladies were next placed in the same order and made to walk the steps; then came the trial for both parties to proceed at the same time while I pushed one here and another there, and all the while singing to myself to assist in their movements. Many of the parents were delighted.
>
> After this first lesson was over I was requested to *dance to my own music*, which I did until the whole room came down in thunders of applause, in clapping hands and shouting. . . . I went to bed extremely fatigued.[16]

Audubon would gladly have stayed in Happyland forever, but he had work to do—and *The Birds of America* to sell. On May 18, 1826, he sailed for Liverpool, England.

6 The Birds of America

Two months at sea, and he had no idea when he would see his family again. When he wasn't seasick, he wrote in his journal, addressing the entries to Lucy as if they were letters. He sketched the sailors on deck and the fish they caught—dolphins, barracudas, sharks. A whale as long as the ship spouted in the waves. And everyone on board watched the horizon for pirates, as attacks were common in those days. But there was still time to worry. Audubon had failed to find a publisher in Philadelphia; what if he failed again? Some days his anxiety took over completely. "I immediately feel chilled, and suddenly throw my body on my mattress . . . , scarce able to hold the tears from flowing."[1]

The ship docked in Liverpool on July 21. The city was smoky and crowded, buzzing with the industry created by its cotton trade with the United States. "My heart nearly failed me," Audubon wrote.[2] He would rather have been surrounded by a flock of birds than a flock of strangers in a foreign land. Lucy's sister Ann was then living in Liverpool with her husband, Alexander Gordon. Audubon rushed to see his relatives, but they acted as if they hardly knew him. "Yet what have I done?" he wrote to Lucy. "Ah, that is no riddle, my friend, *I have grown poor.*"[3]

He rented rooms at an inn, then walked out to present a letter of introduction from a New Orleans businessman to a family named Rathbone. The Rathbones were wealthy cotton merchants and art collectors at the center of Liverpool's cultural life. They gathered around as Audubon, so nervous that he was "panting like the winged Pheasant," untied the strings of his portfolio.[4] One by one he held up his pictures. To his great relief, the Rathbones declared them "splendid" and promised to help him in any way they could.[5] Sixty-five-year-old Mrs. William Rathbone Sr., whom Audubon called the Queen Bee, became the first person to subscribe to *The Birds of America*, and this was before the artist knew if the book would ever be produced.

The Rathbone friendship was the magic key that opened the door to Audubon's life in England. One introduction led to another, and only ten days after arriving in Liverpool, he held his first exhibition. It was a stunning success. Hundreds of people came to gaze at the wild things that belonged to America. There was the bald eagle, America's national bird. The wild turkey, both male and female, with the mother bird leading her babies through the forest. The Baltimore oriole, whose nest dangled from a branch like a soft pouch. The great horned owl, with its tufted ears and bold stare. "Drawn from Nature by J. J. Audubon." These birds were called "a vision of the New World."[6]

America *was* a new world then. Only twenty years before Audubon's exhibit, Meriwether Lewis and William Clark had been on their historic expedition through the American West. One of Lewis's tasks on that trip had been to gather as many new species of plants and animals as he could find. Audubon's century was a golden age for *naturalists*—people who study nature, mostly plants and animals—because there was so much to learn about what the wilderness held. Naturalists, whose

28. *Great Horned Owl.* In *Ornithological Biography*, Audubon tells how he almost died chasing one: "I suddenly found myself in quicksand up to my armpits, and . . . must have remained to perish, had not my boatmen come up and extricated me."

field is called *natural history*, explored the world in search of the rare and the new, and they amassed collections of specimens to study and classify. Their research laid the foundation for the modern sciences of botany, zoology, and biology. The most famous naturalist of the 1800s was Charles Darwin, who would sail to the Galapagos Islands in the 1830s. Audubon was working in the same spirit of discovery. When he started his quest for America's birds, only a small number of them had been pictured or even described.

To the English, Audubon was as exotic as his birds. He slicked his hair back with bear grease and wore woodsmen's clothes, like a character from *The Last of the Mohicans*. Visitors crowded his rooms, and the elite of Liverpool sent their carriages to bring him to formal dinners. In the gleam of candlelight and crystal, he entertained them all. He claimed to have camped out with Daniel Boone. He performed birdcalls and demonstrated the howl of a wolf. Hadn't he ever been attacked by Indians or at least a grizzly bear? his listeners wondered. Well, no, he answered, with a smile. The only creatures that had ever bothered him in the woods were ticks and mosquitoes. The artist found that he had a talent for self-promotion, even though he complained in private of terrible shyness. When he was asked to meet Lord Stanley, an aristocrat who would later become prime minister, Audubon wrote, "all my hair . . . stood straight on end."[7]

In October, he traveled by stagecoach to Edinburgh, the capital of Scotland. One of the first people he met there was a man named William Lizars. After looking at the first few watercolors, Lizars leaped out of his chair. "My God! I never saw anything like this before!"[8]

No one had. Before Audubon, most ornithologists depicted birds in profile and static poses. Their goal was to identify a species and all its

29. *John James Audubon*. Victor and Johnny painted their father in his woodsman's clothes.

30. *Wild Turkey*. The mother and her poults.

characteristics, not to make art. But Audubon had found a way to do both, blending scientific accuracy with color and motion and spirit. He was the first to draw birds going about their daily activities and as they really lived, in mated pairs or larger groups. He was the first to show each stage of life, from newly hatched to very old. He was one of the first to include a bird's whole environment, whether a frog-filled swamp or the outskirts of a town. And he was the first ornithologist to draw all his subjects life-size. In the age before photography, this was the next best thing to being there. One man wrote after seeing Audubon's collection, "A magic power transported us into the forests."[9]

Audubon still hadn't found a publisher, so he and Lizars decided to produce *The Birds of America* themselves. Lizars was a skilled craftsman called an engraver. In the 1820s, *engraving* was the process by which many copies of a picture could be made for use as a book illustration. First the engraver traced a drawing onto a copper plate. Then he used acid to cut the tracings deep enough into the plate to hold ink. After ink was applied, a clean sheet of paper was pressed against the plate in order to receive the impression of the drawing. The result would be a black-and-white print as similar to the original picture as possible. Then the print was ready to be colored by hand.

Audubon and Lizars planned to publish *The Birds of America* in five installments, or "numbers," a year. Each number would include five different species. Subscribers would pay in installments, too, for a total of a thousand dollars. Since Audubon wanted to engrave four hundred species in all, he had set himself an enormous task. Against friends' advice, he insisted that like the drawings, the prints be made life-size. For this, Lizars would have to use special "double elephant" paper—at 29 ½ inches by 39 ½ inches, it was the largest size made. It would be

31. *Whooping Crane*. This crane can grow to be five feet tall.

big enough even for the whooping crane, America's tallest bird, as long as the bird's neck was shown curving downward toward the ground.

While Lizars began the engravings, Audubon was caught up in a storm of work, often getting by on four hours of sleep. He had to prepare his drawings for the engraving process, redoing many with the aid of his memory, which, luckily, was almost flawless. He had to pay all the production costs and support himself at the same time, so he painted dozens of pictures to sell. These were mostly oil paintings, and his subjects were hunting scenes and animals, everything from an otter caught in a trap to a pair of fighting cats. Audubon gave drawing lessons and showed other ornithologists how to use the position board. And to establish himself as a naturalist, he wrote scientific papers and read them at scholarly meetings. For his achievements, royal societies and the finest academic institutions honored him with memberships—"I, merely a Woodsman!"[10]

There was also the never-ending push to sign up subscribers, for without their money, *The Birds of America* would come to a halt. All that winter and at all hours, Audubon's carriage rolled through Edinburgh's snowy streets to exhibitions and meetings and dinners. "My head is like a Hornet's Nest and my body wearied beyond calculations," he admitted.[11] One evening he was so distracted that he went out wearing his bedroom slippers. But he could not afford to stay home.

"It is Mr. Audubon here, and Mr. Audubon there; I only hope they will not make a conceited fool of Mr. Audubon at last," he wrote.[12] In spite of all the attention, he missed his home. "How I wish I was in America's dark woods, admiring God's works in all their beautiful ways."[13] He wrote almost every day to Lucy. Most of the time, he begged her to come to England: "My Dearest Friend— . . . I cannot bear to be without thee."[14] But at other times, he told her to wait until he had saved enough money to support them both. Lucy, who was still teaching in Louisiana, had trouble making up her mind, too. As time passed, she felt more and more abandoned, and her own letter writing nearly stopped.

When Lizars finished the first five prints, Audubon took them to London to rustle up subscribers. He hated England's largest city. It was foggy, dirty, and crime ridden, and it seemed to him "like the mouth of an immense monster, guarded by millions of sharp-edged teeth."[15] He gave money to children begging in the streets and was horrified to hear that three men had been hanged for stealing sheep. "The contrast between the rich and the poor is a constant torment to me," he wrote.[16] Yet he bought himself a new suit—black "like a mournful Raven"—to dine with lords and ladies, famous artists, heads of museums and scientific societies.[17] Distinguished people signed up for his book, including King George IV.

Lizars wrote from Edinburgh to say that his colorists were on strike, and he advised Audubon to find a new engraver. After days of trudging up and down London streets, Audubon met a father-and-son team, Robert Havell Sr. and Robert Havell Jr. The older Havell was a colorist, the younger an engraver. They made a sample print of one of Audubon's birds. When he saw it, he wanted to hug and kiss them but danced around the room instead. The Havells were even better at their work than Lizars. Faster and cheaper, too.

Not everyone idolized the American artist. One aristocrat, the Earl of Kinnoul, called Audubon to his mansion to tell him that his pictures were a "swindle."[18] To the earl, all the birds looked alike. Audubon held his temper in front of "the rudest man I have met in this land."[19] But later, he wrote that the earl looked like a bird himself, "with a face

32. *Bald Eagle*, America's national bird.

like the caricature of an owl."[20] Then came news from Philadelphia that his old enemy, George Ord, was in a fury over scientific papers that Audubon had written. In one Audubon described experiments he had conducted that showed that vultures find their prey by sight, not scent. In another, he claimed that rattlesnakes could climb trees. "Lies," fumed Ord, and he teamed up with an English naturalist named Charles Waterton to try to ruin Audubon's reputation.[21] But these men were "crazed Naturalists of the Closet," countered Audubon.[22] They stayed home and merely read about nature while he, Audubon, went out to see it for himself. In time Audubon's findings on the vulture would be proven largely correct. His paper on the snake, although it contained other errors, was also right: rattlesnakes *can* climb trees.

"I do any thing for money now a days," he told Lucy.[23] In between his stays in the big cities of Scotland and England, he toured the smaller ones, looking for new subscribers and collecting money from old ones. In September 1828 he went to Paris—his first time back to France in twenty-two years. Both his parents were dead now, but his sister, Rose, was still living in Couëron. Audubon did not visit her. Instead he stayed in the city, enjoying French coffee, which he thought was the best in the world, and trying to sell his book. Although he did not sign up many new subscribers, he met with Baron Georges Cuvier, the most respected naturalist in France. Cuvier took one look at Audubon's portfolio and called it "the greatest monument erected by art to nature."[24] Cuvier introduced Audubon to the duc d'Orléans, who would soon become King Louis-Philippe. D'Orléans subscribed to *The Birds of America*, and so did the current French king, Charles X.

Back in London, Audubon concluded, "I have not worked in vain."[25] He had won great praise in Europe. And his "Great Idea," thanks to the Havells' engravings, was on its way to becoming a reality. But by 1829 he had been away from America for three years. His marriage with Lucy was at the breaking point, and he had missed seeing his sons grow from boys to young men. He had more work to do in America, too, with more species to find. On April 1, having left the Havells with enough watercolors to keep them busy for a whole year, Audubon boarded the ship *Columbus* and headed for home. Out on the Atlantic, he thought about the twists and turns his life had taken—"Fortune if not blind certainly Must have his Lunatic Moments."[26] He had left America under a cloud of bankruptcy and failure. He was coming home a star.

7 *Team Audubon*

Audubon did not rush to Louisiana to see Lucy. Now that *The Birds of America* was in production, he was in a race against time to collect as many species as he could. He had begged his wife to understand: "Thou knowest I must *draw hard* from Nature *every day* that I am in America."[1] Everything else, even family, would have to wait. If the 1820s were a storm of activity for him, the 1830s would be a hurricane. In a time when horseback, stagecoach, and steamboat were the main means of travel, he would cover an almost impossible amount of territory. Not only would he make three more trips back and forth across the Atlantic, but he would crisscross North America—east, south, north, and west.

His ship had docked in New York in May, just in time for him to comb the Northeast for birds that had flown up from the South. Back in the woods and the wild again, Audubon was happy. It was the love season, and birds were pairing off and building nests. At Great Egg Harbor on the New Jersey shore, a meadowlark was looking for his mate. To Audubon, it was like a scene from *Romeo and Juliet*:

> The male is still on the wing; his notes sound loud and clear as he impatiently surveys the grassy plain beneath him. His beloved is

not there. His heart almost fails him, and disappointed, he rises toward the black walnut tree, . . . and loudly calls for her whom of all things he best loves.—Ah!—there comes the dear creature; her timorous, tender notes announce her arrival. Her mate, her beloved, has felt the charm of her voice. His wings are spread, and buoyant with gladness, he flies to meet, to welcome her, . . . they place their bills together and chatter their mutual loves![2]

Next Audubon explored Pennsylvania's Great Pine Forest. Remote and unspoiled, it inspired him to write, "There is nothing perfect but *primitiveness*."[3] He spent two weeks in the forest with a lumberman, Jedediah Irish, and his family, eating venison and bear meat, collecting plants and birds, nests and eggs—and drawing. By summer's end, he had a batch of new pictures to send to England for engraving. A Swiss landscape artist named George Lehman painted backgrounds, but still Audubon had so much to do that he wrote, "I wish I had eight pairs of hands."[4]

Not until the birds migrated back down south in the fall did he see his family again. First he stopped in Louisville, where Victor and Johnny were living with their uncle Billy Bakewell. Audubon hardly recognized his sons. Victor was almost twenty; Johnny was sixteen. After the visit, Audubon made his way to Louisiana. The state was then in the grip of a yellow fever epidemic, but he risked exposure to see Lucy. He arrived at the town of St. Francisville, in the West Feliciana country, in the middle of the night: "It was dark, sultry, and I was quite alone. I was aware yellow fever was still raging at St. Francisville, but walked thither to procure a horse. Being only a mile distant, I soon reached it, and entered the open door of a house I knew

33. *Eastern Meadowlark* by John James Audubon.

to be an inn; all was dark and silent. I called and knocked in vain, it was the abode of Death alone! The air was putrid; I went to another house, another, and another; everywhere the same state of things existed; doors and windows were all open, but the living had fled."[5]

At last he found a horse and rode through the woods to Lucy's plantation. "I went at once to my wife's apartment; . . . I pronounced her name gently, she saw me, and the next moment I held her in my arms. Her emotion was so great I feared I had acted rashly, but tears relieved our hearts, once more we were together."[6]

He showed Lucy some of the Havells' engravings and asked for her—and the boys'—help with *The Birds of America*: "We should all go to Europe together and to work as if an established Partnership for Life consisting of Husband Wife and Children."[7] Now that Lucy was reunited with John, her feelings of abandonment melted away, and when she saw what he had accomplished, she agreed to become part of the team. Victor and Johnny liked the idea, too. Soon the three would be almost as busy as Audubon himself. Victor would go to England to collect payments and supervise the engraving process. Johnny would hunt for birds with his father and even draw some of them for the publication. Lucy would copy and edit manuscripts and take care of many business details. The long years of separation were over, and Audubon could proudly say, "We are a Working Familly."[8] In 1830 John and Lucy traveled to Washington DC, where they met with President Andrew Jackson in the White House. Then they sailed to England.

While Robert Havell Jr. turned out one engraving after another (his father had retired), Audubon sat down to write a companion text for *The Birds of America*. Titled *Ornithological Biography*, it would be a collection of short biographies, or "life histories," of every species that the artist drew. The biographies are based on Audubon's close observation—"I write as I see," he had said—and they sparkle with the personality of each bird.[9] Scientific details, such as measurements and taxonomy, are included. *Ornithological Biography* is also sprinkled with the frontier "Episodes," Audubon's stories about everything from a country fair in Kentucky to the ordeal of a man lost in the forest for forty days.

He wrote until he dreamed about birds. He wrote until his fingers puffed up and his muscles cramped. "I would rather go without a shirt or any inexpressibles through the whole of the florida swamps in musquito time than labour as I have hitherto done with the pen."[10]

In Edinburgh, he met a Scottish naturalist named William MacGillivray. In addition to being a friend of Charles Darwin's, MacGillivray was a fine writer and an expert on bird anatomy. Audubon hired him as an editor and scientific adviser. Working around the clock, the two men finished the first volume of *Ornithological Biography* in four months. Lucy patiently copied every word by hand for publication in the United States. Audubon and MacGillivray kept writing the bird histories even when they were apart, exchanging manuscripts and ideas by mail.

The search for America's birds was far from over. Audubon chose Florida for his next ramble. Claimed by Spain for centuries, the Territory of Florida had only joined the United States in 1821 and would not become a state until 1845. In 1831 Audubon toured Florida's east coast with George Lehman and a young taxidermist, Henry Ward. Starting in St. Augustine, they wandered up the St. John's River. The trip was disappointing, yielding too few birds and too many scorpions. According to Audubon, the region was "a garden, where all that is not mud, mud, mud, is sand, sand, sand."[11]

34. *Roseate Spoonbill.* Like other birds with beautiful feathers, this bird was hunted almost to extinction.

But then, on a schooner called the *Marion*, the group explored the southern tip of Florida and the islands off its coast known as the Florida Keys. This journey was worth it. "The sea was of a beautiful, soft, pea-green color, smooth as a sheet of glass," wrote Audubon.[12] The men passed an abandoned shipwreck, saw manatees and giant sea turtles. Once Audubon swam too close to a large shark. At night he dreamed that it was dragging him out to sea. Among flowers and groves of trees, he saw flocks of water birds—flamingos, cormorants, pelicans, and snow-white egrets. "The air was darkened by whistling wings."[13]

By the side of a pond, Audubon shot a white ibis, and it fell to the water with a broken wing. As it struggled to shore, alligators chased it. Audubon tells what happened next:

35. *White Ibis* by John James Audubon.

I was surprised to see how much faster the bird swam than the reptiles, who, with jaws widely opened, urged their heavy bodies through the water. The Ibis was now within a few yards of us. It was the alligator's last chance. Springing forward as it were, he raised his body almost out of the water; his jaws nearly touched the terrified bird; when pulling three triggers at once, we lodged the contents of our guns in the throat of the monster. Thrashing furiously with his tail, and rolling his body in agony, the alligator at last sunk to the mud; and the Ibis, as if in gratitude, walked to our very feet, and there lying down, surrendered itself to us.[14]

He kept the big bird and cared for it. When its wing was healed, he released it back into the wild.

From Florida he went all the way north to Labrador, a peninsula in northeastern Canada. No ornithologist had ever been there before. Eskimos, Canadian fishermen, French fur trappers—only the hardiest people lived there. Even in summertime, when Audubon arrived, the seas were treacherous. Gale-force winds blew, and icebergs glittered off the coast. His traveling companions were four adventurous young men, including his own son Johnny. They all wore mittens, woolen hats, thick trousers, and heavy boots but were still freezing and wet most of the trip.

They sailed from Maine on the *Ripley*. Near Nova Scotia, the *Ripley* approached the famous Bird Rock, which juts four hundred feet above the water. At first Audubon thought that the rock was covered with snow. It wasn't snow, explained a member of the crew, but a colony of seabirds called gannets.

"I rubbed my eyes," wrote Audubon, "took my spy-glass, and in

36. *Northern Gannet*, with the Bird Rock in the distance.

an instant the strangest picture stood before me. They were birds we saw—a mass of birds of such a size as I never before cast my eyes on. The whole of my party stood astounded and amazed. . . . The nearer we approached, the greater our surprise at the enormous number of these birds, all calmly seated on their eggs or newly hatched brood, their heads all turned to windward, and towards us."[15]

The air was swirling with gannets, too, and everyone watched as the birds dived for fish. From heights of more than a hundred feet, they plunged into the water like rockets.

Labrador itself was rocky and wind-torn, dotted with stunted trees and covered in spongy moss. Audubon thought it a land of "wonderful dreariness," except for the millions of birds that came there to breed—ducks, auks, guillemots, gulls, puffins, loons, and more.[16] At forty-eight, he couldn't hike as far as the young men, but he spent seventeen-hour days drawing birds on a table below the *Ripley*'s deck.

Although Audubon shot thousands of birds in his lifetime, he claimed that he never disturbed nesting birds or their eggs. In Labrador, he saw—and instantly despised—the "Eggers," men who raided wild birds' nests and sold their eggs for a living. "At every step each ruffian picks up an egg so beautiful that any man with a feeling heart would pause to consider the motive which could induce him to carry it off."[17] Eggers destroyed whole generations of birds, and Audubon concluded that "this war of extermination cannot last many years more."[18]

By August the storm clouds of winter were already gathering. Audubon had lost fifteen pounds and was exhausted from the rain and cold, the tossing waves. "Seldom in my life have I left a country with as little regret."[19] But he was satisfied that he had learned much that was not known by any other ornithologist either in Europe or America.

In 1837 Audubon looked west to Texas and headed there with Johnny and his friend Edward Harris. Their route took them by stagecoach across Alabama. There they witnessed one of the tragic events in Native American history—the Trail of Tears.

Five Indian tribes—the Cherokees, Choctaws, Chickasaws, Seminoles, and Creeks—had lived in the southeastern part of North America for centuries, long before the United States was founded. But after the American Revolution and into the 1800s, southern states and territories were established. White settlers came and began to covet Indian lands.

In 1830 President Andrew Jackson had signed a law called the Indian Removal Act. It decreed that the southern tribes must be resettled in "permanent Indian Territory" west of the Mississippi River. So tribe by tribe, family by family, Indians were torn from their homes. Taking with them only what they could carry, they endured a forced march westward. Thousands died along the way.

Audubon recorded what he saw:

> 100 Creek Warriors were confined in Irons, preparatory to leaving for ever the Land of their births!—Some Miles onward we overtook about Two thousands of These once free owners of the Forest, marching towards this place under an escort of Rangers, and militia mounted Men, destined for distant Lands. . . . Numerous groups of Warriors, of half clad females and of naked babes, trudging through the Mire . . . the evident regret expressed in the masked countenances of Some, and the tears of others—the howlings of their numerous Dogs; and the cool demeanour of the Chiefs—all formed Such a Picture as I hope I never will again witness.[20]

In New Orleans Audubon's three-man expedition boarded a boat and sailed across the Gulf of Mexico along the Louisiana coast. Although they were tormented by mosquitoes and sweltering heat, they collected a wealth of plants and birds along the way. When they reached Galveston, they were no longer in the United States but the new Republic of Texas. The year before, Texans had won their independence from Mexico and elected Gen. Sam Houston as their first president. (Like Florida, Texas would join the Union in 1845.)

Audubon's group ventured inland to Houston, the capital of the republic, where they met the president himself. Sam Houston wore a velvet coat and trousers trimmed with gold lace, but his presidential mansion was a two-room log cabin. Noted Audubon, "The ground floor was muddy and filthy; a large fire was burning; a small table, covered with paper and writing materials, was in the centre;

camp-beds, trunks, and different materials were strewn around the room."[21] President Houston introduced the visitors to members of his cabinet, "some of whom bore the stamp of intellectual ability."[22] Everyone took a glass of grog and toasted to the future of Texas. It was a visit that Audubon would never forget.

It took longer for Audubon's fame to catch on in America than it had in Europe. And throughout the 1830s, his constant enemies, George Ord and Charles Waterton—those "beetles of darkness"—were hard at work.[23] As volumes of *Ornithological Biography* were published to glowing reviews, Ord and Waterton accused Audubon of not being the real author. "That impudent pretender and his stupid book," Ord wrote.[24] Audubon never responded directly to their attacks, but he told a friend, "I really care not a fig—all such stuffs will soon evaporate, being mere smoke from a Dung Hill."[25]

He was right. Newspapers were reporting on his travels. Philadelphia's Academy of Natural Sciences subscribed to *The Birds of America*, easing Audubon's anger at that city. America's great universities and public institutions—the U.S. Congress and several state governments—signed up as well. Many subscribers were prominent citizens, such as the statesman Daniel Webster and the writer Washington Irving, author of "The Legend of Sleepy Hollow."

By the summer of 1837 *The Birds of America* was almost finished. All Audubon needed now were specimens of birds that two other naturalists, Thomas Nuttall and John Townsend, had collected on their expedition to the American West. The Audubon family was now together in Europe, shuttling between London and Edinburgh in a final push to the finish line. From dream to reality, thought Audubon. "How delicious is the Idea."[26]

37. *Atlantic Puffin* by John James Audubon.

8 *This Strange Wilderness*

From its earliest days, Audubon knew that *The Birds of America* was unique. As it neared completion, he wrote, "I have laboured like a Cart Horse for thirty years on a Single Work, have been successful almost to a miracle in its publication so far, and am thought a-a-a (I dislike to write it, but no matter here goes) . . . a Great Naturalist!!!"[1]

The last number of *The Birds* was published in 1838, twelve years after the first. The entire work was four volumes long and depicted 489 American species, twice as many as Alexander Wilson—or anyone else—had shown before. Some of the family and larger groupings had taken years to assemble, with Audubon using a collage technique to paste several bird drawings onto one sheet of paper. The printed engravings were so faithful to the original watercolors that they made Robert Havell Jr. famous along with Audubon.

One year later, the fifth and last volume of *Ornithological Biography* came out. This work, too, was revolutionary. Audubon had created a new kind of nature writing, combining scientific fact with his exuberant and poetic descriptions. "You may well imagine how happy I am at this moment," he wrote. "I find my journeys all finished, . . . my mission accomplished."[2] The family sailed back to America—this time for good—and settled in New York City. At fifty-four and after so many years of almost superhuman effort, Audubon could finally rest.

Of course, he did not. He immediately began work on the *Octavo* edition, a miniature version of *The Birds of America*. Johnny Audubon helped. Using a device called a camera lucida, Johnny projected the images at one-eighth their original size onto sheets of paper and traced them. The traced drawings were then prepared for publication, not by copper engraving like the originals, but by the process of *lithography*, or etching on stone. The *Octavo* would be published in installments from 1840 to 1844. At the price of a hundred dollars, it was much less expensive than the big bird book, and to Audubon's delight, it became an instant best seller.

Audubon had a friend named John Bachman who was a minister and fellow naturalist. Bachman's motto was "Nature, Truth, and no Humbug."[3] He had been an important member of the team that had helped produce *The Birds of America*, sending from his home in Charleston, South Carolina, specimens and information about the birds of the American South. Audubon's and Bachman's families had merged as well. Johnny Audubon married Bachman's daughter Maria, and Victor married another Bachman girl, Eliza.

In 1840 Audubon and Bachman decided to do for North American mammals what Audubon had done for birds. As with the birds, no complete work had been published on the subject before. It was to be a joint effort—drawings by Audubon, text by Bachman. They chose a title—*The Viviparous Quadrupeds of North America*. (Quadrupeds are four-legged animals. The term "viviparous" refers only to mammals because all mammals except the platypus and the anteater give birth to live babies instead of laying eggs.) But early in the project's

LEPUS AMERICANUS, ERXLEBEN.
NORTHERN HARE.
Winter Pelage.
WINTER.

38. *Northern Hare*, pictured in its winter coat.

planning stages, tragedy struck. Both Johnny's and Victor's wives died of tuberculosis. Audubon had particularly loved Victor's wife, twenty-two-year-old Eliza. He was drawing a hare when she died: "I drew this Hare during one of the days of deepest sorrow I have felt in my life."[4]

Still he kept working. In 1841, with money from the *Octavo*, he bought land for his family—thirty acres on the banks of the Hudson River. That land is now part of New York City's Upper West Side, but it was country then, all grass and tall, old trees. The Audubons named the new place Minniesland, because Victor and Johnny called their mother Minnie.

"Minniesland for ever say I!"[5] Audubon built a large, wooden house—the family's first permanent home since the Kentucky years—with a view of the water and the boats sailing by. Next came a barn and stables, a garden, and fruit trees. The naturalist also gathered around himself a menagerie of wild animals—foxes, elk, deer, even wolves.

His workroom was stacked from top to bottom with drawings, art supplies, and stuffed birds and quadrupeds. At one end of the room was a long drawing table where Audubon sat, preparing for *The Viviparous Quadrupeds*. Sketches of small mammals—rabbits, weasels, moles, mice, and rats—began to pile up.

John Bachman was an expert on mammals. "Don't flatter yourself that the quadrupeds will be child's play," he warned.[6] He counted twenty-four types of tree squirrel alone. And, he added, "books cannot aid you much. Long journeys will have to be undertaken."[7]

"My Hairs are grey, and I am growing old, but what of this? My Spirits are as enthusiastical as ever," wrote Audubon, and he planned a trip out west to see the quadrupeds of the mountains and plains.[8] He knew it would be his last great adventure.

From Minniesland he traveled westward, noting along the way how the once open countryside was filling up with towns and farms. In St. Louis, he climbed aboard the *Omega*, a steamboat belonging to the Chouteau family, which controlled most of the fur trade on the western frontier. Audubon had brought along four others: John Bell, a taxidermist; Isaac Sprague, an artist; Lewis Squires, a young man who would be a general helper; and Edward Harris. According to Audubon, the other passengers were an "extraordinary and motley crew."[9] Most were fur trappers from many different countries who would fan out into the wilderness, trap animals, and sell their pelts at trading posts along the western rivers. Others were Indians, visitors to

39. *Common American Wildcat*. This was Audubon's name for the bobcat, or lynx.

St. Louis, who were heading north and home. As the boat started up the Mississippi, many of the trappers got drunk. They fired their guns in the air—*Pop! Pop! Pop!*—and cheered. The date was April 25, 1843.

When the *Omega* reached the Missouri, it had to fight the churning current, wind through twisting channels, and steer around sandbars and sunken logs. The crew rowed ashore often to chop wood to fuel the boat's engine. When Audubon wasn't busy drawing, he went ashore, too, "in search of quadrupeds, birds, and adventures."[10]

Up and up for hundreds of miles. The travelers passed the Platte River—the path of the Oregon Trail—where wagons trains were just beginning to roll west. They passed the famous Council Bluffs, where

VULPES VELOX, SAY.
SWIFT FOX.

40. *Swift Fox*. Audubon saw many of these fast runners on the prairie.

in 1804 Lewis and Clark had first met with chiefs of the Missouri River tribes. The *Omega* was chugging through the Great Plains now. Indian Country. The vast land that would become the states of Kansas, Nebraska, South Dakota, and North Dakota was not even organized into territories yet, and few Americans had ventured this far. High bluffs lined the river. Behind them the prairie stretched out as far as the eye could see. "We are advancing in this strange wilderness," Audubon wrote, spellbound.[11] Blood-red sunrise and moonlit nights. There were hardly any trees.

In Sioux territory—now South Dakota—they saw hundreds of tipis pitched next to a trading post. They began to see buffalo, too, and

Audubon explored his first prairie dog town. Farther north, in what is now North Dakota, the boat reached a trading post called Fort Clark. The villages of the Mandan Indians were nearby. Audubon toured their round, earthen lodges, and the Mandans toured the steamboat. "There they stood in the pelting rain and keen wind, covered with Buffalo robes, red blankets, and the like, some partially and most curiously besmeared with mud. . . . They looked at me with apparent curiosity, perhaps on account of my beard. . . . They all looked very poor."[12]

They were poor—and so hungry that they ate the rotten meat of drowned buffalo. In 1837 a steamboat had brought smallpox to the Upper Missouri region. The Indians had never been exposed to the disease before and so had developed no immunity to it. A terrible epidemic raced through the tribes, wiping out village after village. The Mandans were hit hard; 90 percent of them died. In his journal, Audubon recorded some desperate stories:

"One young warrior sent his wife to dig his grave. . . . The grave was dug, and the warrior, dressed in his most superb apparel, with lance and shield in hand, walked towards it singing his own death song, . . . and . . . threw down all his garments and arms, and leaped into it, drawing his knife as he did so, and cutting his body almost asunder. This done, the earth was thrown over him, the grave filled up, and the woman returned to her lodge to live with her children, perhaps only another day."[13]

Audubon also told the story of "an extremely handsome and powerful Indian who lost an only son, a beautiful boy, upon whom all his hopes and affections were placed. The loss proved too much for him; he called his wife . . . and said to her, 'Why should we live? All we cared for is taken from us, and why not at once join our child in the

41. *Fort Union Trading Post* by Karl Bodmer.

land of the Great Spirit?' She consented; in an instant he shot her dead on the spot, reloaded his gun, put the muzzle in his mouth, touched the trigger, and fell back dead."[14]

On June 12, the *Omega* reached its final destination of Fort Union, in North Dakota, where the Yellowstone River flows into the Missouri. The hard-working steamboat had set a speed record to get there, traveling two thousand miles in only forty-eight days.

The fort was built to handle trade with the Blackfoot Indians and other Upper Missouri tribes. There they exchanged buffalo hides for the whites' guns, knives, cloth, needles, and more. This was the farthest west Audubon had ever been, and he could not have wished for a wilder place. "Wolves howling, and [buffalo] bulls roaring, just like the long continued roll of a hundred drums."[15] He was given a special room to draw in, and he unpacked for a two-month stay.

The agent in charge of Fort Union was Alexander Culbertson. His wife was a Blackfoot named Natawista. One day the couple put on war paint and staged a horse race. "Mrs. Culbertson and her maid rode astride like men," wrote Audubon, "and all rode a furious race, under whip the whole way, for more than one mile on the prairie; and how amazed would have been any European lady . . . at seeing the magnificent riding of this Indian princess—for that is Mrs. Culbertson's rank—and her servant. Mr. Culbertson rode with them, the horses running as if wild, with these extraordinary Indian riders, Mrs. Culbertson's magnificent black hair floating like a banner behind her."[16]

Audubon's group left the fort daily on horseback to explore. Often they camped out on the prairie, using buffalo dung to fuel their campfires. It was summertime, and there was an astounding number of birds. On the way upriver, Audubon had already named a species each for Bell, Sprague, and Harris. Now he became the first ornithologist to discover that the western meadowlark was a different species than the meadowlark back east.

This was the kingdom of the quadrupeds, too. Antelope bounded over the prairie. Elk bearing huge antlers swam the rivers, and bears foraged in the brush. Wolves prowled everywhere, even coming near the fort at night. Audubon made a special trip to North Dakota's Badlands, home of the bighorn sheep. There, where ancient rivers had carved a strange landscape, the sheep scampered up and down rock towers a thousand feet high.

But the buffalo ruled over all. The shaggy, bellowing beasts were

42. *American Bison or Buffalo*. "Almost every green spot along the hillsides
has its gang of buffaloes," Audubon told a friend.

the largest mammals—viviparous quadrupeds!—on the North American continent. They ranged over the land in herds so immense that Audubon found it "impossible to describe."[17] It had taken one frontiersman six days to ride through a herd.

Audubon shot hundreds of mammals to study and draw for his new book, and he sent home skins and specimens preserved in barrels of brine. He hunted for science, he hunted for food, and he hunted because he loved to. Buffalo hunting was the most exciting—and most dangerous—of all. But Audubon was fifty-eight now, and he had trouble shooting his rifle while riding at a mad gallop. "How I wish I were twenty-five years younger!"[18] And once he was almost gored by a wounded bull, so he watched more often than he took part. After one hunt, he looked on amazed as Natawista scooped out the still-warm brains of a dead buffalo and ate them, raw and dripping.

In spite of his love for hunting, Audubon realized that species could become extinct, and as the years went by, he grew increasingly concerned. He saw that, like the passenger pigeons in Kentucky, buffalo were being slaughtered at an alarming rate: "What a terrible destruction of life, as it were for nothing, or next to it. . . . The prairies are literally *covered* with the skulls of the victims."[19] And he added, "This cannot last; even now there is a perceptible difference in the size of the herds, and before many years the Buffalo, like the Great Auk, will have disappeared; surely this should not be permitted."[20] But the animals continued to be shot for their hides, for their meat, and for sport. By the 1880s—Audubon would not live to see his prediction come true—almost all the buffalo would be gone.

Winter comes early to the Upper Missouri country. By mid-August, there was a sharp bite in the wind, and the air was thick with the coming snows. Audubon and his men built an oar-powered barge called a mackinaw and started for home. The naturalist had not had time to go as far as he had wanted, to the Rocky Mountains and beyond, but he had seen a part of the Wild West and many of its wild creatures.

Down past the Mandan villages and the Sioux encampments, down through the prairie that he called "sublime."[21] From St. Louis he traveled back to New York, reaching Minniesland in November. "Thank God, [I] found all my family quite well."[22] The family was bigger now, too. Victor and Johnny had remarried, and the house was filled with their children. Audubon's hair and beard, all white now, were long, and he had brought back with him a coat trimmed with wolf fur. Johnny painted a portrait of his father, looking like a true western frontiersman.

As soon as his barrels of specimens arrived, Audubon sat down to perfect his drawings. With pencil and ink, he drew every whisker and eyelash. He used watercolor, pastel, and oil paint to show the softness of fur and its many shadings. His quadrupeds would be as lifelike as his birds.

As with the *Octavo*, the quadruped pictures were printed on lithographed plates and colored by hand. Audubon brought sample prints to Washington DC so that members of Congress could see them before buying a subscription. He was shocked at how little the politicians knew about the animals of their own country. "The Great Folks call the Rats Squirrels, the squirrels flying ones, and the Marmots, poor things, are regularly called Beavers or Musk Rats."[23]

By 1845, he had finished half the illustrations for the book. But his eyesight was failing. His mind was beginning to fail, too. After a lifetime of drawing, writing, and exploring, he was nearing the end of his working days. The family team stepped in to help. Victor painted backgrounds and sent specimens to John Bachman as Bachman wrote text. Johnny hunted for more quadrupeds and visited European museums to sketch polar bears and other arctic mammals. When he came home, he completed the other half of the drawings. *The Viviparous Quadrupeds of North America*, with 150 large images, was published in three volumes from 1845 to 1848. It was a landmark of natural history, the most complete record of American mammals of its time.

John Bachman visited his old friend in 1848 and found him much changed. "Alas, my poor friend Audubon! The outlines of his beautiful face and form are there, but his noble mind is all in ruins. It is indescribably sad."[24] By 1850 the artist was spending his time wandering the grounds of Minniesland, withdrawn and silent. There came a day when he did not recognize his son.

Billy Bakewell paid a visit. When Audubon saw his hunting buddy from the old Mill Grove days, he sat up straighter and spoke. "Yes, yes, Billy! You go down that side of Long Pond, and I'll go this side, and we'll get the ducks."[25]

These were his last words. John James Audubon died on January 27, 1851. He was sixty-six years old.

43. *John James Audubon* by John Woodhouse Audubon, c. 1843.

9 *Audubon Then and Now*

"The study of ornithology must be a journey of pleasure," Audubon wrote.[1] His own journey gave us the spectacular *The Birds of America*. It marked the beginning of modern ornithology, too, bringing naturalists out to where the birds really lived, to see and study. Audubon's vision—to erase the boundary between ornithology and art—was realized in his historic achievement. Yet there were times, early in his career, when he feared that he would die unknown.

His life itself is one of the great American adventure stories. A passionate rambler, he tramped across the country from shortly after its founding to the middle of the nineteenth century, when Americans were poised to overspread and settle the continent. He met everyone from frontiersmen to presidents and wandered through a wilderness that was teeming with animals in numbers almost unimaginable today. No artist or naturalist traveled as far or saw as much. His art and writings form a unique kind of travelogue of America when it was new. Audubon had a powerful love for his country, and he understood how fast it was changing. In middle age, he looked back on an earlier trip down the Ohio River:

When I think of these times, and call back to my mind the grandeur and beauty of those almost uninhabited shores; when I picture to myself the dense and lofty summits of the forests, that everywhere spread along the hills and overhung the margins of the stream, . . . when I reflect that all this grand portion of our Union, instead of being in a state of nature, is now more or less covered with villages, farms, and towns, . . . when I remember that these extraordinary changes have all taken place in the short period of twenty years, I pause, wonder, and although I know all to be fact, can scarcely believe its reality.

Whether these changes are for the better or for the worse, I shall not pretend to say.[2]

He was a man of his time and a man ahead of his time—a hunter who could kill a hundred birds in a day and an early environmentalist who worried about the survival of species from birds to buffalo. He probably discovered about twenty-three new bird species, although the exact number is hard to know.[3] Taxonomy in Audubon's lifetime was in its infancy, and today DNA analysis is leading to frequent revisions. Audubon was never able to depict all the North American birds. Ornithologists now count more than nine hundred species. But his gift to the world is greater even than his life's work. It is also the legacy that his work has inspired.

The Audubon Society was founded in 1886 by the naturalist George Bird Grinnell, who was tutored by Lucy Audubon when he was a boy. Today the National Audubon Society includes hundreds of state chapters, nature centers, and sanctuaries. While Audubon the man collected birds, the Audubon Society is dedicated to protecting and preserving them. For the twenty-first-century naturalist, bird watching has replaced shooting, and photography provides the close-ups that John James Audubon craved. The mission has evolved.

The Audubon Society and many other bird and wildlife organizations have inherited John James Audubon's concern for bird species under threat and work to save them by educating the public and advocating for protective laws. Some species, such as the Carolina parakeet and the passenger pigeon, are gone forever. But others that Audubon admired—the whooping crane, the roseate spoonbill, the brown pelican—have been pulled back from the brink of extinction.

Naturalists in Audubon's day worked in isolation, but now the Internet has brought birders together nationwide and worldwide. Websites enable organizations to sponsor global bird counts, track migrations, provide field guides, and play recorded birdcalls. Not only professional ornithologists but citizen-scientists, amateurs, contribute important information. How pleased Audubon would have been to know this, for he was self-taught and a citizen-scientist himself.

He is buried at Trinity Church Cemetery in New York City, not far from Minniesland. A tall monument over his grave is carved with birds and mammals, flowers and leaves.

"In imagination I am at this moment rambling along the banks of some murmuring streamlet . . . while the warblers and other sylvan choristers, equally fond of their wild retreats, are skipping in all the freedom of nature around me."[4]

Appendix

LOOKING FOR AUDUBON AND HIS WORLD

HISTORICAL SITES

John James Audubon Center at Mill Grove, Audubon, Pennsylvania

Oakley Plantation House, West Feliciana Parish, Louisiana

Trinity Church Cemetery, New York, New York

MUSEUMS AND GALLERIES

American Museum of Natural History, New York, New York

The Audubon Gallery, Charleston, South Carolina

Joel Oppenheimer Gallery, Chicago, Illinois

John James Audubon Museum, Henderson, Kentucky

Louisiana State Museum, New Orleans, Louisiana

New-York Historical Society, New York, New York

WILDLIFE SOCIETIES AND AN EDUCATIONAL INSTITUTION

American Birding Association, Colorado Springs, Colorado

Cornell Lab of Ornithology, Ithaca, New York
    allaboutbirds.org and ebird.org

National Audubon Society, New York, New York

Glossary

Bachman, John (1790–1874): An American clergyman and naturalist who helped John James Audubon with *The Birds of America* and *The Viviparous Quadrupeds of North America.*

banding: The process of fastening a band around a bird's leg to enable future identification.

biology: The scientific study of living things, mostly plant and animal life.

Blackfoot: An Indian nation of the Upper Missouri country and Canada.

botany: The scientific study of plant life.

brine: Salted water.

camera lucida: A sketching device that uses a prism and a magnifying glass to project an image onto a piece of paper.

Clay, Henry (1777–1852): A politician and statesman who held office in both houses of Congress, served as secretary of state, and won fame for his efforts to avoid civil war.

Cuvier, Baron Georges (1769–1832): A French naturalist known for major contributions to the fields of comparative anatomy and animal taxonomy.

Darwin, Charles (1809–82): The English naturalist who developed the theory of evolution by natural selection.

engraving: The process of cutting images into a plate, usually copper. In Audubon's time, engraving allowed artwork to be copied and printed for use as illustrations.

flatboat: A boat with a flat bottom and squared ends, used for river travel in the nineteenth century.

forage: To search for food.

French Revolution: The violent upheaval in France, lasting from 1789 to 1799, that replaced the monarchy with a democratic form of government.

Grinnell, George Bird (1849–1938): An American naturalist and writer who helped found the Audubon Society and establish Glacier National Park in Montana.

grog: An alcoholic drink, usually rum.

Harrison, William Henry (1773–1841): Ninth president of the United States, who died thirty days after his inauguration.

Houston, Sam (1793–1863): The general famous for his 1836 victory in the Mexican-American War and who also served two terms as president of the Republic of Texas.

Irving, Washington (1783–1859): A writer of essays, satires, biographies, and fiction who is most famous for his stories "Rip Van Winkle" and "The Legend of Sleepy Hollow."

Jackson, Andrew (1767–1845): A general during the War of 1812, an Indian fighter, and the seventh president of the United States, serving two terms, from 1829 to 1837.

keelboat: A boat with a keel and pointed ends that was used for river travel in the nineteenth century.

Lewis and Clark Expedition: Meriwether Lewis and William Clark led the famous expedition, from 1804 to 1806, up the Missouri River to the Pacific Ocean.

Linnaeus, Carl (1707–78): The Swedish scientist who developed the modern system of taxonomy, naming and classifying plants and animals.

lithography: The process of cutting images into a stone plate and printing them. After the late 1830s, lithography became more popular than engraving for making copies of pictures.

mackinaw: A flat-bottomed boat that can be propelled either by oar power or by sails.

Mandan: An Indian tribe living in North Dakota, along the Missouri River. This tribe was almost destroyed by smallpox in the 1830s.

menagerie: A collection of animals, usually wild ones.

natural history: The study of the natural world's plant and animal life, as well as the earth's geology.

naturalist: One who studies nature, especially plants and animals.

New Madrid earthquake: A series of earthquakes occurring in 1811 and 1812 along the Mississippi River. Felt over a wide area, they are the strongest ever recorded in the region.

Nuttall, Thomas (1786–1859): An English botanist and ornithologist who, along with John Townsend, discovered American bird species during a western expedition from the Rocky Mountains to the Pacific Ocean.

Oregon Trail: The path along the Platte River that pioneers followed during America's period of westward expansion.

ornithology: The study of birds.

quadrupeds: Four-legged animals.

Republic of Texas: After winning independence from Mexico in 1836, Texas became an independent republic. It joined the Union in 1845 as the twenty-eighth state.

Shawnee: An Indian tribe with wide-ranging settlements from Georgia to Ohio during Audubon's time.

Sioux: Also known as the Lakota, a large Indian tribe with many different branches, living from Minnesota to the Dakotas during the nineteenth century.

skiff: A small boat powered either by oar or sail.

smallpox: A highly contagious disease caused by a virus.

species: A distinct group of animals sharing the same basic characteristics and habitat and whose members usually breed only among themselves.

specimen: An individual sample that represents a larger group.

steamboat: A type of boat, powered by steam, that came into use in America in 1807 and revolutionized river travel.

Sully, Thomas (1783–1872): An American artist and one of the leading portrait painters of his day.

taxonomy: The science of the classification of plants and animals.

Townsend, John (1809–51): An American naturalist and ornithologist who accompanied Thomas Nuttall on an expedition from the Rocky Mountains to the Pacific Ocean.

Trail of Tears: Following President Andrew Jackson's signing of the Indian Removal Bill of 1830, Indian tribes from America's southern states were forcibly removed from their homelands and resettled on reservations west of the Mississippi.

tuberculosis: An infectious disease caused by bacteria that usually affects the lungs.

viviparous: An adjective that describes an animal that gives birth to live young as opposed to laying eggs.

War of 1812: The war between America and Britain that lasted from 1812 to 1815.

Webster, Daniel (1782–1852): A lawyer, orator, and statesman who served in both houses of Congress, as well as two terms as secretary of state.

Wilson, Alexander (1766–1813): Born in Scotland, this naturalist and ornithologist achieved fame for his multivolume work, *American Ornithology*.

yellow fever: A highly infectious disease caused by a virus that is transmitted by mosquito bite.

zoology: The scientific study of animal life.

Notes

INTRODUCTION

1. J. Audubon, *Writings and Drawings*, 757.
2. Streshinsky, *Audubon*, 321.
3. J. Audubon, *Ornithological Biography*, 1:x.
4. J. Audubon, *Ornithological Biography*, 2:8.

1. BELOVED BOY

1. J. Audubon, *Writings and Drawings*, 768.
2. J. Audubon, *Writings and Drawings*, 769.
3. J. Audubon, *Ornithological Biography*, 1:v.
4. J. Audubon, *Ornithological Biography*, 1:vi.
5. J. Audubon, *Writings and Drawings*, 759.
6. Olson, *Audubon's Aviary*, 42.
7. J. Audubon, *Ornithological Biography*, 1:vi.
8. J. Audubon, *Writings and Drawings*, 769.
9. J. Audubon, *Writings and Drawings*, 770.
10. J. Audubon, *Writings and Drawings*, 768.
11. J. Audubon, *Writings and Drawings*, 770.
12. J. Audubon, *Writings and Drawings*, 769.
13. J. Audubon, *Writings and Drawings*, 771.
14. J. Audubon, *Writings and Drawings*, 772.
15. J. Audubon, *Ornithological Biography*, 1:v.
16. J. Audubon, *Ornithological Biography*, 1:1.

2. AMERICA, MY COUNTRY

1. J. Audubon, *Ornithological Biography*, 2:53.

2. J. Audubon, *Ornithological Biography*, 2:52.

3. J. Audubon, *Ornithological Biography*, 1:ix.

4. Chancellor, *Audubon*, 24.

5. Streshinsky, *Audubon*, 26.

6. Streshinsky, *Audubon*, 26.

7. J. Audubon, *Writings and Drawings*, 775.

8. Streshinsky, *Audubon*, 45.

9. M. Audubon, *Audubon and His Journals*, 1:11.

10. J. Audubon, *Writings and Drawings*, 782–83.

11. J. Audubon, *Writings and Drawings*, 783.

12. J. Audubon, *Writings and Drawings*, 783.

13. Arthur, *Audubon*, 37.

14. Arthur, *Audubon*, 37.

15. J. Audubon, *Writings and Drawings*, 784.

16. J. Audubon, *Ornithological Biography*, 2:8.

3. THE AMERICAN WOODSMAN

1. J. Audubon, *Writings and Drawings*, 785.

2. J. Audubon, *Writings and Drawings*, 786.

3. Olson, *Audubon's Aviary*, 20.

4. J. Audubon, *Writings and Drawings*, 534.

5. J. Audubon, *Writings and Drawings*, 535.

6. J. Audubon, *Writings and Drawings*, 535.

7. J. Audubon, *Writings and Drawings*, 786.

8. Chancellor, *Audubon*, 70.

9. Arthur, *Audubon*, 65.

10. M. Audubon, *Audubon and His Journals*, 1:44.

11. J. Audubon, *Writings and Drawings*, 785.

12. M. Audubon, *Audubon and His Journals*, 1:44.

13. J. Audubon, *Writings and Drawings*, 787–88.

14. J. Audubon, *Writings and Drawings*, 526.

15. J. Audubon, *Writings and Drawings*, 527.

16. J. Audubon, *Writings and Drawings*, 527.

17. J. Audubon, *Writings and Drawings*, 528.

18. J. Audubon, *Writings and Drawings*, 789.

19. M. Audubon, *Audubon and His Journals*, 2:234.

20. M. Audubon, *Audubon and His Journals*, 2:235.

21. M. Audubon, *Audubon and His Journals*, 2:235.

22. J. Audubon, *Writings and Drawings*, 266.

23. Olson, *Audubon's Aviary*, 180.

24. Arthur, *Audubon*, 121.

25. J. Audubon, *Writings and Drawings*, 791.

26. J. Audubon, *Writings and Drawings*, 791.

27. Streshinsky, *Audubon*, 100.

28. M. Audubon, *Audubon and His Journals*, 1:47.

4. DOWN THE MISSISSIPPI

1. J. Audubon, *Writings and Drawings*, 792. Emphasis in original.

2. J. Audubon, *Writings and Drawings*, 792.

3. M. Audubon, *Audubon and His Journals*, 1:37.

4. J. Audubon, *Writings and Drawings*, 785.

5. Olson quotes Audubon in *Audubon's Aviary*, 316.

6. Chancellor, *Audubon*, 82.

7. J. Audubon, *Writings and Drawings*, 3.

8. J. Audubon, *Writings and Drawings*, 520.

9. J. Audubon, *Writings and Drawings*, 21.

10. J. Audubon, *Writings and Drawings*, 67.

11. Arthur, *Audubon*, 115.

12. J. Audubon, *Writings and Drawings*, 72.

13. J. Audubon, *Writings and Drawings*, 72. Emphasis in original.

14. J. Audubon, *Writings and Drawings*, 76.

15. J. Audubon, *Writings and Drawings*, 100. Emphasis in original.

16. Arthur, *Audubon*, 170.

17. J. Audubon, *Writings and Drawings*, 69.

18. Arthur, *Audubon*, 183. Emphasis in original.

19. J. Audubon, *Writings and Drawings*, 83.

20. Arthur, *Audubon*, 183.

5. ON THE WING

1. J. Audubon, *Writings and Drawings*, 145.

2. J. Audubon, *Writings and Drawings*, 756. Emphasis in original.

3. Sanders, *Audubon Reader*, 13.

4. Arthur, *Audubon*, 206.

5. Olson quoted Audubon in *Audubon's Aviary*, 51.

6. J. Audubon, *Writings and Drawings*, 231.

7. J. Audubon, *Writings and Drawings*, 128.

8. J. Audubon, *Writings and Drawings*, 129.

9. J. Audubon, *Writings and Drawings*, 130.

10. J. Audubon, *Writings and Drawings*, 138.

11. Arthur, *Audubon*, 260.

12. Arthur, *Audubon*, 260.

13. Ford, *John James Audubon*, 139.

14. Arthur, *Audubon*, 270.

15. Streshinsky, *Audubon*, 321.

16. Arthur, *Audubon*, 293. Emphasis in original.

6. *THE BIRDS OF AMERICA*

1. Streshinsky, *Audubon*, 162.

2. J. Audubon, *Ornithological Biography*, 1:xiv.

3. Streshinsky, *Audubon*, 164. Emphasis in original.

4. Chancellor, *Audubon*, 118.

5. Chancellor, *Audubon*, 117.

6. Olson, *Audubon's Aviary*, 37.

7. Chancellor, *Audubon*, 120.

8. Foshay, *John James Audubon*, 75.

9. Herrick, *Audubon the Naturalist*, 1:359.

10. Arthur, *Audubon*, 333.

11. J. Audubon, *Writings and Drawings*, 801.

12. Chancellor, *Audubon*, 133.

13. M. Audubon, *Audubon and His Journals*, 1:235.

14. J. Audubon, *Writings and Drawings*, 803–5.

15. Herrick, *Audubon the Naturalist*, 1:377.

16. Herrick, *Audubon the Naturalist*, 1:397.

17. M. Audubon, *Audubon and His Journals*, 1:254.

18. M. Audubon, *Audubon and His Journals*, 1:284.

19. M. Audubon, *Audubon and His Journals*, 1:284.

20. M. Audubon, *Audubon and His Journals*, 1:284.

21. Ford, *John James Audubon*, 296.

22. J. Audubon, *Writings and Drawings*, 847.

23. J. Audubon, *Writings and Drawings*, 808.

24. Arthur, *Audubon*, 369.

25. Chancellor, *Audubon*, 122.

26. Arthur, *Audubon*, 55.

7. TEAM AUDUBON

1. Streshinsky, *Audubon*, 243. Emphasis in original.

2. J. Audubon, *Ornithological Biography*, 2:85.

3. Chancellor, *Audubon*, 161. Emphasis in original.

4. Herrick, *Audubon the Naturalist*, 1:426.

5. M. Audubon, *Audubon and His Journals*, 1:62.

6. M. Audubon, *Audubon and His Journals*, 1:63.

7. Streshinsky, *Audubon*, 255.

8. Streshinsky, *Audubon*, 304.

9. Sanders, *Audubon Reader*, 11.

10. Corning, *Letters of John James Audubon*, 2:50.

11. Herrick, *Audubon the Naturalist*, 2:22.

12. M. Audubon, *Audubon and His Journals*, 2:348.

13. M. Audubon, *Audubon and His Journals*, 2:364–65.

14. J. Audubon, *Writings and Drawings*, 428.

15. M. Audubon, *Audubon and His Journals*, 1:360.

16. M. Audubon, *Audubon and His Journals*, 1:386.

17. M. Audubon, *Audubon and His Journals*, 2:409.

18. M. Audubon, *Audubon and His Journals*, 2:411.

19. M. Audubon, *Audubon and His Journals*, 1:428–29.

20. J. Audubon, *Writings and Drawings*, 840.

21. Herrick, *Audubon the Naturalist*, 2:164.

22. Herrick, *Audubon the Naturalist*, 2:164.

23. Chancellor, *Audubon*, 199.

24. Ford, *John James Audubon*, 296.
25. Herrick, *Audubon the Naturalist*, 2:142.
26. J. Audubon, *Writings and Drawings*, 836.

8. THIS STRANGE WILDERNESS

1. Corning, *Letters of John James Audubon,* 2:136.
2. Herrick, *Audubon the Naturalist*, 2:187.
3. Herrick, *Audubon the Naturalist*, 2:261.
4. Foshay, *John James Audubon*, 118.
5. Streshinsky, *Audubon*, 343.
6. Herrick, *Audubon the Naturalist*, 2:211.
7. Herrick, *Audubon the Naturalist*, 2:209.
8. J. Audubon, *Writings and Drawings*, 855.
9. J. Audubon, *Writings and Drawings*, 594.
10. J. Audubon, *Writings and Drawings*, 598.
11. J. Audubon, *Writings and Drawings*, 588.
12. J. Audubon, *Writings and Drawings*, 615.
13. J. Audubon, *Writings and Drawings*, 642.
14. J. Audubon, *Writings and Drawings*, 643.
15. J. Audubon, *Writings and Drawings*, 732.
16. J. Audubon, *Writings and Drawings*, 677.
17. J. Audubon, *Writings and Drawings*, 725.
18. J. Audubon, *Writings and Drawings*, 591.
19. J. Audubon, *Writings and Drawings*, 692–93.
20. J. Audubon, *Writings and Drawings*, 712.
21. Streshinsky, *Audubon*, 351.
22. J. Audubon, *Writings and Drawings*, 749.
23. Foshay, *John James Audubon*, 120.
24. M. Audubon, *Audubon and His Journals*, 1:76.
25. Ford, *John James Audubon*, 422.

9. AUDUBON THEN AND NOW

1. J. Audubon, *Writings and Drawings*, 758.
2. M. Audubon, *Audubon and His Journals*, 2:206–7.
3. Olson, *Audubon's Aviary*, 63.
4. J. Audubon, *Ornithological Biography*, 2:14.

Bibliography

Arthur, Stanley Clisby. *Audubon: An Intimate Life of the American Woodsman*. Gretna LA: Pelican Publishing, 2000.

Audubon, John James. *Audubon in the West*. Compiled and edited by John Francis McDermott. Norman: University of Oklahoma Press, 1965.

———. *Ornithological Biography, or An Account of the Habits of the Birds of the United States of America*. Volumes 1–5. Memphis: General Books, 2012.

———. *Writings and Drawings*. Edited by Christopher Irmscher. New York: The Library of America, 1999.

Audubon, Maria R. *Audubon and His Journals*. 2 vols. New York: Dover Publications, 1994.

Chancellor, John. *Audubon*. New York: Viking Press, 1978.

Corning, Howard, ed. *Letters of John James Audubon, 1826–1840*. 2 vols. Boston: The Club of Odd Volumes, 1930; New York: Kraus Reprint Co., 1969.

Ford, Alice. *John James Audubon*. Norman: University of Oklahoma Press, 1964.

Foshay, Ella M. *John James Audubon*. New York: Harry N. Abrams, 1997.

Herrick, Francis Hobart. *Audubon the Naturalist: A History of His Life and Time*. 2 vols. New York: Dover Publications, 1968.

Olson, Roberta J. M. *Audubon's Aviary: The Original Watercolors for "The Birds of America."* New York: Skira Rizzoli Publications and New-York Historical Society, 2012.

Sanders, Scott Russell, ed. *Audubon Reader: The Best Writings of John James Audubon*. Bloomington: Indiana University Press, 1986.

Streshinsky, Shirley. *Audubon: Life and Art in the American Wilderness*. New York: Villard Books, 1993.

Illustration Credits

FIG. 1: Collection of The New-York Historical Society (1863.17.211). Digital images created by Oppenheimer Editions. FIG. 2: Collection of The New-York Historical Society (1863.17.47). Digital images created by Oppenheimer Editions. FIG. 3: Tyler Collection, John James Audubon Museum, in Henderson, Kentucky. FIG. 4: Collection of The New-York Historical Society (1863.18.7). Digital images created by Oppenheimer Editions. FIG. 5: Oil on canvas mounted on panel, 20 x 30 inches. Godel & Co., New York; photographer: Allan Tarantino. FIG. 6: Collection of The New-York Historical Society (1863.17.120). Digital images created by Oppenheimer Editions. FIG. 7: Collection of The New-York Historical Society. Digital images created by Oppenheimer Editions. FIG. 8: Collection of The New-York Historical Society (1863.17.1). Digital images created by Oppenheimer Editions. FIG. 9: Collection of The New-York Historical Society. Digital images created by Oppenheimer Editions. FIG. 10: Collection of The New-York Historical Society. Digital images created by Oppenheimer Editions. FIG. 11: Photo by Denis Finnin. Image # 1498, American Museum of Natural History, Library. FIG. 12: From the Archives of the Museum of Comparative Zoology, Ernst Mayr Library, Harvard University. FIG. 13: Collection of The New-York Historical Society (1863.17.406). Digital images created by Oppenheimer Editions. FIG. 14: John James Audubon Museum in Henderson, Kentucky. FIG. 15: John James Audubon Museum in Henderson, Kentucky. FIG. 16: Collection of The New-York Historical Society (1863.17.62). Digital images created by Oppenheimer Editions. FIG. 17: Collection of The New-York Historical Society (1863.17.324). Digital images created by Oppenheimer Editions. FIG. 18: Collection of The New-York Historical Society (1863.17.68). Digital images created by Oppenheimer Editions. FIG. 19: Collection of The New-York

Historical Society (1863.17.26). Digital images created by Oppenheimer Editions. FIG. 20: Collection of The New-York Historical Society. Digital images created by Oppenheimer Editions. FIG. 21: Collection of The New-York Historical Society (1863.18.30). Digital images created by Oppenheimer Editions. FIG. 22: Collection of The New-York Historical Society (1863.17.137). Digital images created by Oppenheimer Editions. FIG. 23: Collection of The New-York Historical Society. Digital images created by Oppenheimer Editions. FIG. 24: Collection of The New-York Historical Society (1863.17.102). Digital images created by Oppenheimer Editions. FIG. 25: Collection of The New-York Historical Society (1863.17.21). Digital images created by Oppenheimer Editions. FIG. 26: Collection of The New-York Historical Society (1863.17.32). Digital images created by Oppenheimer Editions. FIG. 27: Collection of The New-York Historical Society (1863.17.76). Digital images created by Oppenheimer Editions. FIG. 28: Collection of The New-York Historical Society (1863.17.061). Digital images created by Oppenheimer Editions. FIG. 29: Photo by Denis Finnin. Image # 1822, American Museum of Natural History, Library. FIG. 30: Collection of The New-York Historical Society (1863.17.6). Digital images created by Oppenheimer Editions. FIG. 31: Collection of The New-York Historical Society (1863.17.226). Digital images created by Oppenheimer Editions. FIG. 32: Collection of The New-York Historical Society (1863.17.31). Digital images created by Oppenheimer Editions. FIG. 33: Collection of The New-York Historical Society (1863.17.136). Digital images created by Oppenheimer Editions. FIG. 34: Collection of The New-York Historical Society (1863.17.321). Digital images created by Oppenheimer Editions. FIG. 35: Collection of The New-York Historical Society (1863.17.222). Digital images created by Oppenheimer Editions. FIG. 36: Collection of The New-York Historical Society (1863.17.326). Digital images created by Oppenheimer Editions. FIG. 37: Collection of The New-York Historical Society (1863.17.213). Digital images created by Oppenheimer Editions. FIG. 38: Oppenheimer Field Museum Edition (plate 12), courtesy of Oppenheimer Editions. FIG. 39: Oppenheimer Field Museum Edition (plate 1), courtesy of Oppenheimer Editions. FIG. 40: Oppenheimer Field Museum Edition (plate 52), courtesy of Oppenheimer Editions. FIG. 41: Fort Union On The Missouri, Karl Bodmer, Aquatint/Engraving, ca. 1839–49, Montana Historical Society, X1970. 27. 09. FIG. 42: Oppenheimer Field Museum Edition (plate 57), courtesy of Oppenheimer Editions. FIG. 43: Image # 2A12973, American Museum of Natural History, Library. FIG. 44: Collection of The New-York Historical Society (1863.17.313). Digital images created by Oppenheimer Editions.

Index

Queen Bee (Mrs. William Rathbone, Sr.), 50

Rabin, Jean-Jacques, 1. *See also* Audubon, John J.
Rabin, Jeanne (mother), 1
rambling: early love of, 2; in Kentucky, 17. *See also* expeditions
Rathbone, Mrs. William, Sr., 50
red-shouldered hawk, *47*
Ripley (ship), 68
roseate spoonbill, *66*
Rozier, Ferdinand, 13–16, 17, 21
ruby-throated hummingbird, *xx*

subscribers, 55, 57, 60, 72
swift fox, *79*

taxidermy, 65
taxonomy, 13; Carl Linnaeus, founder of modern, 18

Texas, travels to, 70, 71
Townsend, John, 72
trumpeter swan, *21*

Viviparous Quadrupeds of North America, The, 75, 77–86, *85*

warbler, 36
Ward, Henry, 65
Waterton, Charles, 72
white ibis, 66, *67*, 68
whooping crane, *56*, 57
wildcat. *See* common American wildcat
wild turkey, *14*, *54*
Wilson, Alexander, 18, 30; criticism of, 46

yellow-breasted chat, *38*, *40*
yellow fever, 62